How To Transform Yourself

From Employee To Online Entrepreneur

"Escaping the 9 to 5 Wage Slave Syndrome"

By

Omar Johnson

This book is dedicated to my son Nadir, my daughter Jelania and my wife Yolanda and it is inspired by my mother Flora Johnson. May you rest in peace.

Table of Contents

Introduction 5

Chapter 1- My Story 8

Chapter 2 – How Did You Ever Become an Employee in the First Place? 35

Chapter 3: The Employee Mindset Vs The Entrepreneur Mindset 43

Chapter 4 – Changing Your Mindset – The Transition 62

Chapter 5-Your Money Blueprint and Changing The Way You Think About Money 99

Chapter 6 -Why Be An Online Entrepreneur?. 102

Chapter 7 – Online Business Essentials 115

Chapter 8- Online Business Models 140

Chapter 9: Funding Your Online Startup 172

Chapter 10: Don't Quit Your Day Job Just Yet 177

Conclusion 186

Introduction

So tell me how did you ever allow yourself to become a 9-5 wage slave toiling minute by minute, hour by hour, day by day producing products and services for someone else and in the process making them rich while you settled for the crumbs?

Have you ever even given it a thought? Probably not. Why? It's because you're too busy running on the J.O.B. hamster wheel going nowhere fast in your life as a dutiful employee.

By the way J.O.B. stands for "just over broke". I know you're probably thinking "how do you know that I'm broke, you don't even know me?" Well I don't need to know you personally, but what I do know is that 46% of the people in the United States die broke. According to an MIT research study nearly half of retirees die with savings of $10,000 or less and 19% of Americans die with "zero" financial assets.

And if you're thinking about social security carrying you through your retirement years forget about it. These statistics bear witness to that statement. The average monthly Social Security check taken from a pool of 53 million beneficiaries was $1,066. Can you see yourself spending your "Golden Years" living on that amount? Sadly, 1 out of 4 Americans will depend completely on Social Security as their primary retirement source.

Let's forget about retirement for a second and let's look at the current state of the economy. Overall, are jobs being produced or eliminated? Can you say that you will be at the current job that you presently have in the next 7 years? Heck, let's not even stretch it out that long how about the next year or month? You can't say right? The reason for your uncertainty is because the state of the economy is very fragile.

People are losing their jobs left and right. The official unemployment rate is 9% however the real unemployment rate is about 20% and what happens to people who solely depend on a j.o.b. for food and shelter when they can't sincerely find work? You guessed it they become homeless or they apply for food stamps to feed themselves.

In fact, 15% of all Americans receive food stamps. According to the statistics there are 46.37 million people receiving food stamps through the Supplemental Nutrition Assistance Program.

Don't get me wrong I'm not completely bashing the idea of working a 9-5 job mainly because my mother and father worked for others to support our family and I'm pretty sure that you are working a 9-5 if not for the same reason then it's for a similar noble reason. However, that's not why you picked up this

6

book. You picked up this book because you want to make a change. You want to design a new and prosperous reality.

Hey I'm not even encouraging you to quit your day or night job, that would be foolish of me, but what I am encouraging you to do is think and act outside of the 9-5 wage slave box to achieve financial freedom for yourself and your loved ones.

This book will show you how to accomplish that goal by analyzing your current employee mindset and juxtaposing it with the mindset of an entrepreneur with the aim of showing you the mindset and actions that you need to adopt to transition yourself from being an employee to being an online entrepreneur.

Chapter 1- My Story

My fascination with entrepreneurship began at an early age and was heavily influenced by the exploits of my mother Flora Johnson. My mother grew up in rural South Carolina during the Jim Crow era where opportunities were far and few for black people. However, she believed that the only way to tackle and solve this dilemma was to acquire more knowledge, further her education and relocate to another state.

She correctly recognized that more opportunities were opening up in the north so she migrated to New York City where she met and married my father and produced three children which consisted of my two brothers and me. While raising us she attended Baruch College in New York City where she obtained a B.S. degree in accounting. After graduating from Baruch College she attended Long Island University where she obtained her Master's degree in taxation. I can vividly and fondly remember accompanying my mother to her classes when she was attending Long Island University and patiently waiting outside of her classroom while she received her instructions from her professors.

I also remember being rewarded for my patience with a slice of cheese cake from the world famous Junior's restaurant which was located down the block from the University.

What I find to be amazing was while my mother was working to complete her Master's she was working as an accountant and simultaneously raising us at the same time.

After completing her Master's degree she continued to work as an accountant at various accounting firms most notably she worked at the major accounting firm Price Waterhouse. However, as time went on my mother basically soured on employee life. She voiced her displeasure for us to hear how she grew tired of working for incompetent bosses, missing out on promotions and working late hours without getting rewarded for it.

The one that thing that I most admired about my mother was that when she was dissatisfied with something she changed it. It didn't matter how challenging or difficult achieving that change might be she went for it without hesitation. I inherited this trait from her.

Understanding that true independence and financial freedom comes strictly from self reliance my mother ultimately decided to make that change by jumping into the entrepreneurial waters by starting her own accounting business. She successfully built her business from scratch and had many prominent people as clients.

I tell you the story of my mother because she was the impetus and the foundation for my entrepreneurial pursuit and endeavors. I intently watched and observed her actions and learned many valuable lessons. Plus, she was my biggest supporter. She passed away and is no longer with us. She passed on her incredible legacy of entrepreneurship and self determination to my brothers as well as her grandchildren.

My Entrepreneurial Beginnings

My first foray into entrepreneurship began in my freshman year while attending Wagner College, a private college located in Staten Island, New York. I created a company called Unique Sounds and basically what I did was sell music "mix tapes" to anyone who would buy them. I had two turntables, a D.J. mixer some records and I was in business. This stint was short lived because I really didn't have the time to devote to it as I was too busy with my studies and playing Division 1 basketball at Wagner.

Even though this business was short lived I learned some important and valuable lessons from it, mainly how to market, price and sell a product. What I learned about marketing was how to determine who my target audience was for my "mix tapes". I decided that the quickest way to sell them was to target the people who knew of me. Not necessarily because of my music exploits, but knew of me from playing basketball or attending school with them.

I started off by targeting the people I went to prep school with at Worcester Academy in Massachusetts. My prep school yearbook contained the names and addresses of the students who graduated in that particular year. I sent out a sales letter to each one of them describing the contents of my mix tape as far as the songs and artist's that were included. I also offered them the opportunity to purchase it at the discounted price of $12 if they sent a check or money order in before the deadline date that I stated in the sales letter.

The response was great and I received a great deal of orders. From the process of selling my mix tapes to the people that I went to prep school with I learned the importance and value of having a mailing list of prospects to market your product to. I also learned the valuable skills of copywriting, how to craft a killer sales letter, how to price a product and how to get people to feel a sense of urgency and take action within a specific time frame by giving them a deadline. These are all valuable skills that you need to have and know how to do if you want to be a successful entrepreneur.

During this time period (1984) there wasn't any internet or ecommerce as we know it today so I could not market my mix tape via online marketing. Not to say that I would have because I soon realized that although the idea of selling a music mix tape seemed innocent to me, it was actually against the law to sell other people's copyrighted music. So that was basically the end of my mix tape entrepreneurial venture.

While in college I majored in accounting and no doubt I was heavily influenced by my mother because I like the fact that she used her knowledge of accounting to build a business and I figured I would do the same. One of the requirements to receive an accounting degree was I also had to take other business courses in addition to my accounting courses. I took courses like marketing and management.

As part of my extracurricular learning I also began to read magazines like Forbes, Fortune, and Success and I quickly discovered by reading those magazines that what I was "learning" about marketing and business in college was drastically different from the way real life entrepreneurs viewed and executed marketing and business in building their companies from the ground up.

I came to the conclusion that what I was learning in school was only preparing me for the life it was meant to prepare me for, "employee life". The courses that I took were designed to teach me just enough so that I could be a functional employee in a corporation, nothing but a cog in somebody else's machine. It's no wonder why a majority of those uber famous and fabulously wealthy entrepreneurs find it absolutely necessary to drop out of college. I guess they saw the writing on the wall.

I can only imagine Bill Gates at Harvard listening to some professor who is making no more than $60,000 a year teach him about how the world works and how to get a product out to the marketplace. In fact, here's a who's who list of famous entrepreneurs who dropped out of college or never completed their "education".

Bill Gates – Multibillionaire who dropped out of Harvard during his sophomore year to found Microsoft with his childhood friend and fellow multibillionaire Paul Allen who also dropped out of Washington State University after 2 years.

David Geffen – Multibillionaire founder of Geffen records and DreamWorks dropped out of college after only completing one year.

Mark Zuckerberg – Multibillionaire founder of Facebook dropped out of Harvard in his sophomore year after the company that he founded in his dorm room began to take off.

Steve Jobs – The late Apple founder dropped out of Reed College after just six months. He also founded Pixar and is known for creating such stellar products as the Ipod, Iphone, Ipad and the Mac computer.

Henry Ford – The late multibillionaire founder of the Ford Motor Company did not attend college at all.

Michael Dell – Multibillionaire founder of Dell Computer which he started in his dorm room dropped out of the University of Texas at Austin during his freshman year.

Ralph Lauren – Multibillionaire fashion designer studied business for two years at Baruch College before dropping out.

Ray Kroc – Founder of the McDonald's franchise, did not even attend college and dropped out of high school.

As I write this I ponder the thought whether I would have dropped out of college if a company that I started while in school began to take off? The answer is a resounding yes. I would have dropped out in a heartbeat. Some opportunities only come around once in a lifetime and I believe that you have to be ready to pounce when that opportunity presents itself.

For example, if Bill Gates didn't leave Harvard at the precise moment that he did to start Microsoft someone else would have started a similar company and filled that void that existed in the marketplace. Gates timing, foresight and business acumen enabled him to seize the opportunity and dominate the entire world with his software.

So since I didn't "see" any such opportunity for me while attending college and the N.B.A. wasn't calling, I graduated from Wagner with a B.S. degree in accounting. Then I hit the job market which culminated in me working at various jobs as an accountant for several years which to me was boring stuff. In many ways I utterly detested my life as an employee mainly because it was mundane and predictable. Plus, I disliked being confined to a desk all day long and taking orders from some bozo. I didn't like the idea that I had to pay my dues to rise up the corporate ladder to make more money. I wanted to control my own destiny and build my own ladder.

My entrepreneurial spirit began to take hold of me more and more as I read about and witnessed the success of people who decided to take the entrepreneurial dive. I knew that I wanted to be an entrepreneur since my mix tape experience, but I didn't know exactly what path to take. Starting a full fledge accounting business was out of the question simply because I found accounting to be rather boring. Plus as an accountant all I really did in essence was count other people's money. Heck, I wanted to make and count my own money.

Starting an online business wasn't an option during this time (1989-1990) because the internet was just in its early stages of development. In fact, the World Wide Web didn't exist so my choices at that time were to either open up a brick and mortar store or supply some type of product to brick and mortar operations. I chose the latter, because opening up a brick and mortar store would have been an expensive and difficult task. I eventually decided to start a record company called Xtra Large Records.

I started this record company based on my familiarity with hip hop music plus my brother Malik was one of the true pioneers of this genre of music. He recorded the hip hop classic K-Rob versus RammellZee produced by the late great and world famous Jean Michel Basquiat. My brother also at a later date went on to produce several records for rap mogul Jay Z and his record label Rocafella records.

So musically and sonically I was covered because I had my brother on board as a producer. The problem was I did not have any artists signed to my label at the time. So I did the next best thing to get my record label off the ground, I recorded a record myself which was produced by my brother. It was a two sided single and on side A there was a song entitled "Hit The Note" and on side B there was a song entitled "I Could Make You Move To This".

I didn't really have a stage name so I used my real name. I just put a period after each letter (O.M.A.R.). I even convinced my mother to invest in this venture and I still have the actual check that she wrote to get the project off the ground. I started off by selling the records that I manufactured throughout the streets of New York City guerrilla style. Our small team literally walked the streets of New York City with a boom box playing the record for all who would stop and listen and try to convince them to purchase it. We were hustling New York City style.

We eventually began to sell the record to record stores throughout the New York City metropolitan area as well as other parts of the country via consignment and straight up cash. I got the names and telephones numbers of the various record stores from the BillBoard Record Retailer Directory and I began calling those record retailers one by one. The record was selling well despite receiving virtually no major radio airplay. However, we were able to get some radio play from some college radio stations and a few underground hip hop radio shows. At one of these college radio stations I even did an interview alongside the late great hip hop legend Tupac Shakur.

Meanwhile I began looking for ways to sell more records and scale the business. I contacted various independent record distributors and most of them purchased my record outright in bulk and the others paid me for what was sold after 45 days. As a result of distribution I sold 5 times the amount of records that I sold previously prior to distribution and I sold them a lot faster. I even sold records to different countries such as Japan, The United Kingdom, Germany and Canada.

From this experience I learned the power of distribution and how you make a lot more money quicker by plugging into an already existing and established system or platform that contains hungry buyers that you did not have to spend any of your own money on in terms of marketing to attract. You are simply serving the role as a supplier of the product and the creator or owner of that system and platform charges you a small toll for each sale that you make. When I eventually decided to become an online entrepreneur the two platforms that I plugged into and sucked money out of consistently were Ebay and Amazon. I'll tell you more about that a little later.

After the initial release of my record I went on to release many records by others that also included other genres of music most notably dance music. I did this for several years until the economics of the business didn't make sense anymore. The margins were real thin and although I sold a decent amount of records from each release none of them became major hit records.

Eventually the business became unsustainable and I had to pull the plug on it. All was not lost though, because I learned some valuable and priceless lessons from this entrepreneurial experience and the main one was never get into a business where the margins are razor thin unless there is some sort of lucrative and high profit margin back-end sale.

Back-end sales are sales that you make after the first sale to the customer. The first sale that you make to a customer is known as a front-end sale. Most savvy marketers that use a back- end strategy usually offer a front-end product that has value and price that front-end product at a very enticing low price. The intention is to make the first sale so that the customer can develop some sort of confidence and trust from buying from you. Once this is established most of the barriers of offering a high price product on the back-end are removed and the end result is a sale, if the product is something that they will benefit from.

Once I pulled the plug on my record label I realized I was certifiably unemployable. By that I mean I was an entrepreneur at heart and I did not have an employee mindset or spirit. I thought about entrepreneurship 24 hours a day and really couldn't picture myself working for someone else because I hadn't for years, but the money started to run out.

It wasn't like I smoothly transitioned from one entrepreneurial venture to the next so I began to do some independent consultant work as an accountant for a little while then

I reluctantly returned to work as a 9 to 5 employee.

Meanwhile in 1993 the internet began to really take shape. Marc Andreessen and Eric Bina who were assistants at the National Center for Supercomputing Applications (NCSA) at the University of Illinois created the Mosaic web browser. A web browser if you don't know already is a software that allows you to access the internet, visit websites and do activities within them like logging into a site, viewing multimedia, sending and receiving email etc. On your desktop computer your browser would be Internet Explorer, Firefox, Chrome or some other application.

Most of the browsers that existed before Mosaic were Unix machines which were expensive. So at that time the web was mostly used by academics and engineers who had access to Unix machines. In addition, the user interfaces of those original browsers were not user friendly which hindered the spread of the web. The Andreessen and Bina created Mosaic browser totally changed the game because it was super user friendly and more graphically sophisticated.

Its popularity and usage skyrocketed and the web exploded. It became the new frontier similar to the California gold rush of 1848. Although initially I wasn't part of this new frontier just yet I watched it very closely. Of course I wasn't the only one watching as the internet grew a whopping 341,000% in one year.

The dot com era was in full swing. Internet companies were popping up all over the place. Companies with little or no revenue were getting insane market valuations. Knowing a little bit about history this reminded me of the tulip mania that occurred in Amsterdam in the 1600's when people began speculating on the tulip flower and a tulip exchange was established. Citizens of Amsterdam began trading their land, life savings and anything of value so that they could liquidate and buy more tulips.

Entrepreneurs of all ilk flocked to this new goldmine of an opportunity called the internet. Jeff Bezos left his job at a hedge fund company called D.E. Shaw and started Amazon in his garage. When the CEO of the hedge fund company tried to talk Jeff Bezos out of quitting by basically telling him he would be a fool to leave a high paying secure job, Bezos told him this was something he had to do. The internet at this time he pointed out was growing at 2400% per year and he would rather try and fail at a startup than never try at all. Just like Bill Gates, when Bezos saw the opportunity to be a dominant player in the marketplace he pounced on it without hesitation.

Pierre Omidyar was another important entrepreneur that took full advantage of the opportunity that the internet offered by founding Ebay. Just like Bezos he was an employee who worked for a company called General Magic, but he left after the money he was making from Ebay outstripped his salary and as they say the rest is history.

Meanwhile back at the ranch I was learning everything I could about the internet while I was working 9-5, which mainly included learning how to build a website and ways to market online. I was also studying ways how to suck money out of existing platforms such as Ebay in particular, because this auction site was capturing the imagination of the public and people flocked to it by the millions to buy and sell items. Ecommerce was in full effect.

I was fast becoming an expert on how the internet worked and I surmised that there would be a ton of people out there who could benefit from my expertise so I set up shop, built a website and began an internet consulting business. Revisiting the California gold rush of 1848, if I were living in that gold rush era I would have been that entrepreneur who would have quickly realized that since people would be digging for gold there would be a need and a high demand for shovels. I would have been the person who supplied the shovels to the populace while also digging for gold. During this internet boom I was providing the equivalent of a shovel in the form of being a helpful resource to others while also mining for my own internet riches.

My internet consulting business immediately took off and the revenue poured in. I correctly identified that there was a strong segment of the marketplace who wanted to know "How To"; how to build a website, how to get visitors to a website, how to position a website in the search engines etc. At this particular time Google didn't exist, people relied on search engines like Excite and AltaVista which was the Google of its time.

Every day it seemed liked the internet grew by leaps and bounds and as it grew, I grew along with it. The technological advances were rapid and astounding. One of the advances that was made was the vast improvement of security and encryption with payment systems. What was hindering ecommerce somewhat at this time was consumer's lack of confidence in the security of their private information when making a purchase online.

They were absolutely terrified and rightly so, that someone would hijack their personal information like their name, address, telephone number and credit card information and use it nefariously. People were really spooked and back then it seemed like every instance of online fraud was highlighted by the mass media, which further exacerbated the problem. As internet security in this area became much stronger consumer confidence grew and with the price of the desktop computer dropping down to more affordable prices ecommerce soared.

Other technological advances like the invention of the PDF file by Adobe and MP3 audio allowed me to scale my internet consultant business to new heights, because instead of just doing one on one consulting, by email, in person, or by telephone, I was able to deliver information digitally to my clients and potential clients over the internet. Later on, I further scaled the business by creating information products in mass in the form of e-books and home study courses.

The Dot Com Bubble Burst Ebay and Amazon Emerge

During the late 1990's and early 2000's the dotcom era produced a massive bubble then that bubble finally burst. The stock market corrected itself as most internet companies were obscenely and grossly overvalued. For example, during this time E-Toys an online toy retailer was considered more valuable than Toys-R-Us even though Toy-R-US had more revenue and profits.

Many internet companies simply disappeared into the thin air. However, out of this rubble the two companies that I had been paying close attention to Ebay and Amazon, emerged. People couldn't get enough of Ebay and fast forward in a few short years it grew into a multibillion dollar company. I was already experiencing the phenomenon of Ebay as a buyer, but it was time for me to extract money out of it as a seller and an entrepreneur and I did just that. I plugged into their platform.

Initially I couldn't think of anything that I could sell, then a light bulb went off in my head and I gave my mother a call to find out if she had any belongings that she wanted to discard. She gave me a lot of brand name things she no longer had any use for: Gucci handbags, Gucci shoes, designer clothes etc. and one by one I listed these items for sale on Ebay and that's how I humbly began as a seller on Ebay.

All of those auctions sold quickly and I was elated. However, I soon ran out of things to sell, so I did some extensive research on what was hot and selling on Ebay. This led me to selling brand name clothing, which I also successfully sold and did extremely well with. As I dug more into my research analyzing other sellers on Ebay, I came to the conclusion that the sellers who were selling a lot of items and making a lot of money couldn't have been buying all of those items using their own money, unless they were an established retail or wholesale brick and mortar operation that already did business this way.

Then I stumbled upon how these sellers were doing it. They were using dropshipping, a secret method at the time that was not known to many. With dropshipping you don't have to use any of your own money to purchase products for resale. It requires no stocking of inventory and there are no upfront costs. This in a nutshell is how dropshipping worked for me as a seller on Ebay. I simply located wholesalers who offered dropshipping as an option. Once I decided on the products that I wanted to sell from the dropshipper wholesaler's website I copied the images and descriptions of those items (which you are allowed to do), marked them up and listed them for sale on Ebay.

When the items sold and the customers paid me, I used part of those proceeds to order the product from the wholesaler and to also pay for the shipping cost to the customer. Now of course the shipping cost wasn't coming out of my pocket, because when the customer bought the product from me on Ebay, they also had to pay for the cost of shipping. Along with the payment to the wholesaler, I also forwarded the customer's name and address. The wholesaler then shipped that item to the customer in my name. The remaining money that was left offer was my profit.

Selling items on Ebay using dropshipping became a goldmine for me. I was selling all sorts of electronics, gizmos and gadgets basically because there was little to no risk involved. I blew the lid off the cover and began selling items on Ebay by the boatload. In no time Ebay anointed me with its prestigious and coveted "Powerseller" status.

If you plan on selling products as online entrepreneur from your own website or through platforms like Ebay, Amazon or any other venue and you don't want to run through your precious cash, you should consider utilizing dropshipping. Zappos.com in the beginning built their company by dropshipping shoes to customers. If dropshipping was viable for Zappos in building their business, it can also be viable for you in building your business.

Ebay became my personal ATM machine and I perfected the art and science of selling on it. I even created my own personal Ebay money making selling strategies which included the following: "Find a Thirsty Crowd Strategy", "Second Drink Strategy", "Micro Targeting Strategy", "Karate Chop Strategy", "It's Used But So What Strategy", "The Refurb Strategy", "The Big Profit Strategy" and "The Option Strategy". You can learn about these strategies and the full story on how I make money on Ebay in my book entitled **The Secrets of Making $10,000 on Ebay in 30 Days.**

Pretty much everything I was doing on the internet was working. I was on fire, so naturally my 9-5 job working as an accountant became toast. I simply walked into my

employer's office after my lunch break and
without fanfare announced that I was done and
that marked the end of my life as an employee.
I was no long a 9-5 wage slave.

It's remarkable how Amazon was one of the
few companies to survive the dotcom bubble
burst. Its margins were thin during that time
and that still holds true today and it had yet
to show a profit. The stock price tumbled to
around $4 a share and the pundits started
referring to Amazon as "Amazon dot bomb", but
CEO Jeff Bezos still marched relentlessly
ahead as most visionary entrepreneurs do in
challenging times.

At that time the only way to plug into
Amazon's platform and suck money out of it was
by being an affiliate. As an Amazon affiliate
each time that you drove traffic to their site
and it resulted in a sale you would get paid a
small commission. Amazon relied heavily on
affiliates to get the word out about their
company and drive traffic to their site. In
fact, this is how they rapidly built their
business. Personally, I wasn't interested in
becoming an Amazon affiliate because it wasn't
very appealing to me.

During this particular time period Amazon
primarily sold books and I did not see how I
could make any real money promoting low price
books so I sat on the sidelines, but I still
kept my eyes on Amazon. As time progressed I
watched Amazon grow from selling just books to

selling every imaginable product under the sun to become the largest online retailer in the world. As an entrepreneur I was looking for a way to plug into this behemoth of a platform.

Then one day I tuned into the Oprah Winfrey show and watched and listened as Jeff Bezos unveiled a device called the Kindle. Although I knew instantly that the Kindle was a revolutionary device I can't say that I knew it would take the world by storm in just a few short years. I came to the conclusion that people are usually ingrained in their habits and I didn't think they would give up reading books the traditional way in favor of reading them on an electronic device. Boy was I ever wrong as the Kindle took the world by stormed and disrupted the entire book publishing industry from top to bottom.

People easily adapted and became accustomed to reading their books digitally on the Kindle. Amazon sold millions of Kindle devices. The explosion of the Kindle drove the final nail in the coffin of the Borders book chain as their revenues plummeted even further and they eventually went out of business. Sales and revenue began to also plummet at the venerable Barnes and Noble chain of book stores and they tried to counter with their own electronic reading device the Nook to no avail.

As an entrepreneur I was watching this all play out and hoping that the flood gates of opportunity would open up and it did. Amazon had millions of customers who owned Kindle devices and sensing the need to have more content for these Kindle users Amazon launched the Kindle Direct Publishing program. This platform enabled independent authors and publishers to upload and make available for sale their books in a Kindle format on the Amazon website. This was a revolutionary development because no longer did authors have to take the traditional route in getting their books published.

Traditionally, the way an author brought a book to the marketplace was by first signing with a literary agent who would then shop that author's book to the various big name publishers like Random House, Simon and Schuster etc. This was basically the only way for a book to get on bookshelves at the various bookstores.

As you can imagine with this being the only route of distribution for authors, (besides selling books from the trunk of a car) the book publishing companies wielded an enormous amount of power. They had their choice of what they deemed to be the "pick of the litter" in terms of authors and books. So essentially as an author, if you signed a book deal with a publisher you were "in" and if you didn't sign a book deal with one you were "out".

The Kindle and Amazon's creation of the Kindle Direct Publishing program totally changed the game by eliminating the middle man. Authors no longer had to go through a book publisher to get their books distributed and Amazon made it possible so that you didn't need your book to be in a brick and mortar bookstore to reach the masses.

The Kindle Direct Publishing program represented an irresistible opportunity for me as an online entrepreneur and I dove into it head first, not as a one book author but as a publisher of many books. To date I have published a total of 37 books and out of those 37 books I have personally authored 27 of them. I became an Amazon best-selling author and soon after I plugged into two other Amazon platforms for selling books; CreateSpace which is a print on demand entity for paperback books and ACX which is a platform that distributes audio books to Audible.com, Amazon and the Itunes Music store.

I began to sell thousands upon thousands of books in a short period of time without ever having my book in a traditional book store. What's even better than that is the royalty payments that I receive every month from the aforementioned Amazon platforms for the sale of my books in the Kindle, paperback and audio book formats. Amazon to their credit also revolutionized the royalty percentage that an author receives from sales of a book.

For example, if an author or an independent publisher prices a book between $2.99 - $9.99 Amazon pays out a 70% royalty rate excluding certain conditions. This is revolutionary because authors who are signed to a traditional publishing house normally receive a royalty rate that ranges between 7% - 15% for each book sold, which obviously is dramatically much lower than the royalty rate received when self publishing on Amazon.

Conversely, royalty rates paid by Amazon's subsidiary Audible.com for books distributed through Amazon platform ACX are not too shabby either. If you choose to be distributed exclusively through them (ACX) then your royalty rate starts of at 50% and can escalate as high as 90% depending upon how many units you sell.

Speaking of sales, the reason why I sold so many thousands of books so fast is because I took the time out to understand and master how the Amazon ecosystem works in terms of selling books. I discuss in detail how the Amazon ecosystem works specifically in regards to Kindle books in my book **How To Promote Market And Sell Your Kindle Book.** I also discuss in detail how to effectively scale a book to new heights in another book I wrote entitled **Audiobook Profits: How To Make Money By Turning Your Kindle, Paperback and Hardcover Book Into Audio.**

As I end this particular chapter of my story on how I became an entrepreneur, I must say in all actuality the story really never ends because the online world is constantly evolving and radically changing at a rapid pace which will result in more opportunities for me to grow and spread my online entrepreneurial wings even further. The secret to capitalizing on the opportunities that are presented is by providing value to others as well as the marketplace.

For instance, when Google became the preeminent and most used search engine on the planet and search engine visibility became a must for those who were conducting business online, I mastered search engine optimization and learned how to get a website to rank high for its main keywords on Google as well as the other major search engines like Yahoo and Bing. I created an SEO company based on this unique expertise called GetSeobacklinks.com and offered this valuable service to the marketplace.

I also continue to advise and coach aspiring entrepreneurs who want to succeed online as well as offline through my Entrepreneur Mentorship program. You can receive more information about this program by visiting www.makeprofitseasy.com.

My serial entrepreneurism is not just relegated to the online world. I am a real estate investor as well as a real estate coach who has helped many others succeed. I hope by sharing my story and giving you an inside look at my personal transformation from being an employee to being an entrepreneur you have learned some things that you can apply and utilize for your own transformation.

Transforming yourself from a 9-5 employee to an online entrepreneur may come easy to you or it may represent a challenge. Regardless of your particular case, it will still require you to put in effort and work. So having said that let's begin the process of your transformation.

Chapter 2 – How Did You Ever Become an Employee in the First Place?

So the question begs how did you ever become an employee? You weren't born an employee. You were born in the universe with natural instincts given to you by God or the Supreme Being. It doesn't matter what your religion is, this is not a religious discussion, but you were born with certain natural instincts.

No one taught you how to cry as a baby, you just instinctively knew how to do it and when to do it. When you were hungry you let your mother know that you needed to be fed by crying. Same thing when you soiled your diapers and they needed changing or when you were sick you let others know that you were uncomfortable by crying.

When it was time for you to sit up no one taught you how to sit up and when to sit up, you did that instinctively too when the time was right. You didn't have any concept of what a job was. So how did you get to the point where you are now as a "9 to 5" employee? Let me explain your genesis. You were socialized and conditioned to believe that's what were supposed to do, work for others.

You played games as a child and you pretended to be a "doctor", a "nurse", a "fireman", a "police officer" etc. The idea of being an employee and working for others was also reinforced by your parents and the schools and institutions that you attended. They asked you questions like "what do you want to be when you grow up?" and they beamed with pride and smiled approvingly when you responded "When I grow up I want to be a doctor or a nurse or a fireman or a dentist. You saw their approving expressions when you gave them your answer and you instantly felt accepted and loved because with your answer you made them proud.

As you journeyed through the educational system you were instructed by both your parents and teachers to get good grades because it would enable you to get a good job as an employee. You embraced that concept wholeheartedly and why not? Most people you saw that were considered to be successful in society were employees and worked for someone else.

Eventually, you too joined the workforce as an employee trading hours for dollars. Your life is predictable and you know your daily routine inside out. You get up in the morning everyday to make that trek to the office or where ever you work just to get a few measly bucks so that you can pay your bills, buy a couple trinkets and take a vacation or two.

You figured out a long time ago that you could never get rich working for someone else.

Hell, you even realized that it is only so high you can go in income on your job because the wages are capped unless your pay is directly tied to the amount of business that you bring in. But of course you probably won't have a job like that because you want to have that certainty of making a certain dollar amount per day, per week and per year. The bottom line is you want to know that your check will be there every Friday or every other Friday or whatever day it is that you receive your paycheck. This represents security for you.

You work for medical benefits, 401k's, deferred compensation and hopefully a pension at the end of your employment road, which basically represents the reward that you receive for devoting your entire life toiling for someone else and making them rich. What I am saying to you probably sounds a little bit harsh but hey it's the truth. Can you handle the truth? If you answered in the affirmative let's move forward with the discussion.

The current American education system and its curriculum were designed to make you an employee. In fact, it was modeled after the Prussian educational system which was compulsory and instituted by the Prussian aristocracy to control the masses. Its central goals were the following:

1. To create obedient workers for the mines.
2. To create obedient soldiers for the army.

3. To create well subordinated civil servants for the government.
4. To create well subordinated clerks for the various industries.
5. To create a population who thought the same way about major issues.

Nothing in the 19th century Prussian education system encouraged independent and critical thinking. The American educational system also rewards uniform thinking and conformity. Case in point, to get an "A" in a subject all you really have to do is regurgitate on the test exactly what the teacher or text book has taught you.

If you give answers on the test that are contrary to what the teacher and text book have taught you to believe, you will receive an "F" or a failing grade. So regardless if it's fact or fiction everyone is strongly encouraged to think and act the same way and if they don't they will get severely penalized.

Here is another vivid example. The American school system teaches you in school at an early age that Christopher Columbus discovered America. This would be fine if there weren't any inhabitants on the land already but there was. There were the "Native Americans" or the aboriginal people already present inhabiting and flourishing on the land.

In school, they even tell you that the Native Americans were present when Christopher Columbus arrived, but if you put as your answer on the test that the Native Americans really discovered America and in your argument you stated: How could Christopher Columbus possibly have discovered America when people were already present, you will get a failing grade and get chastised for giving the "incorrect" answer.

And if you keep giving the so called "incorrect" answers the consequences get much more severe. You will be left behind in school and if you start to daze off in class and get fidgety because you are discouraged by what they are teaching you, you will get diagnosed as being hyperactive or suffering from attention deficit disorder. They may even recommend to your parents that you take Ritalin or some other psychotropic drug to control you.

So the question begs why did America adopt the Prussian educational system for its school system? The answer is quite obvious. To get the same results as the Prussian educational system which was designed to produce compliant non-independent thinkers who never questioned "authority" and did as they were told and provided cheap labor for the ruling class.

In fact in 1903, John D. Rockefeller created and funded the General Education Board to take control of the educational system in America. The aim of the General Education Board was similar to the goals and aims of the Prussian educational system instituted by the Prussian aristocracy which was organizing children and creating reliable, predictable, and obedient citizens who worked for them.

To give you solid proof that this is a statement of actual fact, here's what the Reverend Frederick T. Gates, Business Advisor to John D. Rockefeller Sr., wrote in 1913 in The Country School of Tomorrow, Occasional Papers Number 1:

"In our dream we have limitless resources, and the people yield themselves with perfect docility to our molding hand. The present educational conventions fade from our minds; and, unhampered by tradition, we work our own good will upon a grateful and responsive rural folk.

We shall not try to make these people or any of their children into philosophers or men of learning or of science. We are not to raise up among them authors, orators, poets, or men of letters. We shall not search for embryo great artists, painters, musicians. Nor will we cherish even the humbler ambition to raise up from among them lawyers, doctors, preachers, statesmen, of whom we now have ample supply."

So basically you now have a clear understanding why most people become and remain employees, it is simply because they have been indoctrinated by an educational system that is solely designed to make them just that. Furthermore, the employee concept gets reinforced as the ideal concept for economical survival by our parents, friends, families, institutions etc.

Entrepreneurship is not promoted in the school system as a means of controlling your economic and financial destiny simply because it represents financial freedom, independent thinking and the escape from the 9 to 5 wage slave syndrome.

So don't be surprised when you tell people that you are going to be an entrepreneur and you are met with resistance, criticism and perhaps even laughter, because it's a type of reality that a lot of people can't wrap their mind around. Be prepared because you will be met with opposition from family members, friends, and even your significant other. When you say to them adamantly "I'm going to be an entrepreneur" you will hear responses such as "that's too risky", "what about your job?", "how are you going to support yourself if things don't work out?", "make sure that you have a Plan B" etc.

Address their concerns if you must, especially in the case of your significant other, but don't let them discourage you from pursuing a new reality that doesn't consist of being an employee collecting a paycheck at a 9 to 5 job. Don't let them beat you down and don't surrender to them. If they want to choose the so called "security" of a 9 to 5 job which is basically an illusion over freedom then let them.

You have made your choice now have the courage and the intestinal fortitude to stand behind it. I'm not saying that the ride might not be a little bit bumpy along the way, but when you're absolutely committed to being a successful entrepreneur you see the "bumps" as just blips on the screen and nothing more than an opportunity to build your character, sharpen your sword and to ultimately be victorious.

Chapter 3: The Employee Mindset Vs The Entrepreneur Mindset

To transform yourself from an employee to an entrepreneur you have to have a clear understanding of what the mindset of an employee is versus what the mindset of an entrepreneur is. First of all let's define what a mindset is. A mindset is universally defined as a habitual or characteristic mental attitude that determines how you will interpret and respond to situations.

When you transition to being an entrepreneur you can't respond to situations regarding your business like you would as an employee, because not only would it be ineffective, but it would probably result in instant failure.

Having said that let's compare and contrast the mindset of an employee versus the mindset of an entrepreneur.

An employee trades labor for dollars whereas an entrepreneur creates passive income.

An employee has to provide labor to an employer in order to receive a paycheck and if an employee doesn't work he or she doesn't get paid. As an employee it is your responsibility to work when your employer tells you to be there, not when you want to do it. It is because of this very reason that most people work 40 hours or more per week.

An entrepreneur creates passive income. Passive income is income that is not earned by work. It is income that is generated from cash flowing assets. A perfect example of passive income is the royalty payments that I receive from the sale of this particular book. Passive income enables you to make money even while you sleep.

It can be created in many different ways online as well as offline and the best part about passive income is that it is not tied to your time. Here are a few ways you can create passive income as an online entrepreneur.

- Affiliate Marketing
- Selling products via dropshipping
- Kindle book publishing
- Selling on Ebay
- Selling on Amazon

An employee follows direction, is told what to do and executes the vision of the employer while an entrepreneur is self directed, marches to his own drum and is a visionary who utilizes the talent and time of others to make their vision a reality.

When you make that transition from being an employee to being an entrepreneur you have to understand that you are now the boss. You are responsible for creating a vision for your business and formulating a plan that will enable that vision to become a reality.

Instead of following the orders of others as you did as an employee, you now have to become the consummate leader who issues instructions and directions to others. You have to be the one that makes sure that everyone you employ or utilize to perform tasks executes those tasks with the utmost precision because your success as an entrepreneur depends on it.

The bottom line is that the buck starts and stops with you literally.

An employee expects that when they show up to a job and punch the clock they will get paid for the time that they spent working, while an entrepreneur knows that he or she will only make money when they have provided value to the marketplace and there is an actual demand for their products or services.

As an entrepreneur you can't just show up to work and expect to get paid like an employee does. You not only have to work harder, but in most cases especially in the beginning you have to forego paying yourself a salary until your business gets off the ground and starts flourishing.

Even when your business starts to flourish, it is important and absolutely necessary that you reinvest a good percentage of the profits that you make back into the business so that you can continue to grow and expand it.

An employee looks forward to the weekend while an entrepreneur looks forward to every day.

An employee looks forward to the weekend and they say things like "Thank God It's Friday". They dread Mondays and refer to Wednesdays as "hump day" as in they are getting over the hump, while an entrepreneur looks forward to each and every day of the week and the challenges that awaits him or her.

An entrepreneur unlike an employee does not have a job description. He or she does whatever the situation calls for.

As an entrepreneur you wear many hats and plug many holes. For example, if you don't have the benefit of hiring a bookkeeper or an accountant to keep track of your receipts and expenditures, then you have to do it yourself while also performing other important functions like marketing, lead generation, selling, formulating strategies etc.

An employee doesn't have that type of mindset and they are only willing to do what's in their "job description" or whatever they were hired for. If you insist that they perform tasks outside of their job description then they expect a raise or an increase in salary as well as a promotion.

Employees put their destiny in the hands of others while entrepreneurs control their own destiny.

An employee gives up control and places their financial destiny in the hands of the employer simply because they fear the unknown and lack the confidence to strike out on their own. An employee sees starting an untested business as a risky proposition that offers no guarantees or security so they rather cling to the idea and the concept of receiving a steady paycheck and the illusion of security.

An entrepreneur on the other hand embraces taking calculated risks when starting or forming a new business because it allows them to control their own destiny and it represents the freedom to do as you want and please with no restrictions and no limitations unlike a job, especially in terms of how much money you can make.

Entrepreneurs have the courage to strike out on their own and realistically expect to encounter obstacles and challenges along the way, but they have the supreme confidence that they can overcome any and all obstacles and challenges.

Employees get taxes automatically deducted from their pay by the Federal, State and Local government before actually receiving their paycheck while entrepreneurs are allowed to make profits first and pay their taxes last.

Unless you are an investment banker at Goldman Sachs or another such entity you could never get rich as an employee unless you have some meaningful and significant equity in a company. There are two main reasons for this. Number one they will never pay you enough so that you can become rich and number two you can't shield the income that you earn from taxes.

In fact, the federal, state, and local government gets paid first before you ever receive your paycheck and if you doubt this statement just take a look at your pay stub, it clearly shows you who got paid first before you even received your paycheck.

It is nearly impossible for you to create wealth as an employee because you are the last one to get paid. As a matter of fact, you have to work first before you get paid while an entrepreneur gets paid first before they do the work.

Also the federal, state and local government allows the entrepreneur to pay their taxes last and the entrepreneur gets to deduct business expenses against their income to reduce their tax liability. This makes it easier for the entrepreneur to become rich and create wealth.

Conversely, an employee dreadfully looks at taxes as something they don't have control over and something that everyone must pay while an entrepreneur studies and analyzes the tax code looking for creative ways to reduce their tax burden. An entrepreneur also uses and exploits the tax code to become and stay rich.

Entrepreneurs create jobs while employees look for jobs and work at them.

Entrepreneurs create jobs and the following statistics bear witness to my assertion. Entrepreneurs accounted for a whopping 65 percent of the new jobs created between 1993 and 2009. That represents 9.8 million new jobs added to the economy as the result of entrepreneurs creating them. Entrepreneurs create more jobs in our economy than the federal government. They are the engine that drives the economy.

Employees don't create jobs they look for them and work at them. More than likely the job that an employee has was created by an entrepreneur.

Entrepreneurs can pass their business on as a legacy or inheritance onto their children while employees are not able to transfer their jobs as a legacy or inheritance to their children.

Entrepreneurs build and grow businesses and they incorporate their spouse and children into their business and when the time is right the business is passed on to their children who then pass it onto their children and so on.

Entrepreneurs are primarily interested in creating and building a legacy with the sole purpose of passing that legacy onto their heirs. A perfect example of this is Sam Walton passing the Wal-Mart Empire onto his children after he passed away.

Employees are unable to do this. They can't pass their jobs onto their children because they don't own it. All they can do is pass on the ideal of working hard for someone else as their legacy. Harsh, but it's the unfortunate truth. Upset about it? Then become a successful entrepreneur and position yourself to pass your legacy onto your heirs.

An employee's progress is halted by a "glass ceiling", while an entrepreneur can go as far as his or her imagination and vision allows.

No matter where an employee works at or works for they will inevitably encounter a "glass ceiling". They will reach a point in their career or job where they can't go up the ladder any higher. There is only one CEO at a company not two, three or four and even if an employee does reach the position of being a CEO there are no more rungs in the ladder left to climb.

In addition, rising to the top of the corporate ladder takes such an inordinate amount of time, valuable time that it's simply not worth it. Why spend 25-35 years of your precious life trying to be the CEO of a company when you can be a CEO instantly when you start your own business as an entrepreneur?

An entrepreneur does not encounter a "glass ceiling" like an employee does simply because an entrepreneur is not trying to climb up somebody else's ladder. In fact, if there is a ladder you better believe that the entrepreneur built it and owns it.

An entrepreneur can go as far as their mind, spirit and vision allows them to. The possibilities are endless and limitless for the entrepreneur.

Dedicated employees work long hard hours to get the job done while dedicated entrepreneurs use the tool of leverage to build their companies.

Entrepreneurs use the tools of leverage to build and accomplish great things with their businesses. They effectively and efficiently use other people's time, other people's money and other people's skills to rapidly advance their cause and execute their business plan.

So leverage in a nutshell means you are profiting from the efforts of others. With leverage you are able to do more and accomplish more. The more leverage you use, the less you have to work and the more money you make.

One example of using leverage is using the bank's money to purchase a real estate investment. Say that a property cost $300,000 and you put down $10,000 and a bank financed the balance of $290,000 which allows you to purchase the property. That is using leverage, you used very little of your money and the majority of the bank's money to purchase the property.

To give you an example relevant to the topic of online entrepreneurship say that you wanted to start a business selling various e-books, home study courses, and audio programs on different topics on your website. You would use leverage in the form of getting other people to create that content for you. For example, you can go hire freelancers from sites like elance.com, freelancer.com, odesk.com or guru.com and get them to write the e-books, home study courses and record the audio for you. Something that would probably take you months to do if you were doing all the work yourself can be accomplished in just a little bit of time (probably 1 to 2 weeks) by just using leverage. Leverage equals speed.

As an employee you probably used some form of leverage, but it wasn't leverage that was created by you. The leverage was created by your employer when they built a system to facilitate their business. You were hired to be a replaceable part of that system. That's right the system that was built was designed to work with or without you. That's why when employees are fired they are just replaced by new employees and the business doesn't miss a beat.

As an employee you work long hours to complete the tasks assigned to you by your employer however, to effectively make the transition to being an entrepreneur it is essential that you use the tools of leverage to build and grow your business.

An employee believes that school is over once they have completed high school or college while an entrepreneur believes that school is always in session.

School is always in session for the entrepreneur. Just because they completed their formal education (high school, college etc.) doesn't mean that school or the learning process is over. In reality, it has only just begun. You will find entrepreneurs reading books, attending seminars, workshops or doing whatever it takes to enhance or refine their business acumen.

Employees for the most part think differently. They believe that they finished school long time ago. If it isn't something that they need to learn pertaining to their job or getting a promotion most simply aren't interested in extracurricular learning.

Employees are afraid to make mistakes while entrepreneurs see mistakes as hidden opportunities.

Mistakes are inevitable in life, the workplace and in the business world, however employees are deathly afraid of making mistakes because making a mistake may lead to them being chastised or fired from a job. The fear of making a mistake paralyzes their ability to act and kills the employee's spirit of self initiative. That's why most employees play it safe and remain and stay in safe mode. They'd rather be "safe" than sorry.

Now entrepreneurs expect to make mistakes because they know that mistakes are part of the learning and growth process. To the entrepreneur mistakes are nothing more than potential opportunities masked behind perceived setbacks or miscues.

Do you know how many "mistakes" Thomas Edison made on his way to inventing the light bulb? Plenty! The only way to find out if something is going to work or not is to test it or try it out. You go with your gut instinct and make a decision and if that decision turns out to be erroneous, you have the ability to make it right or correct it.

Your decisions are not etched in stone and you are allowed to change your mind and your direction. Bill Gates of Microsoft initially thought that the internet would take a long time to catch on so he didn't focus on it. However, when he realized that he had been mistaken in his belief about the internet, he immediately reversed course and had the entire company focus on the internet so that Microsoft could become one of the preeminent and dominant players on it.

This segues perfectly into the next analysis of the employee versus entrepreneur mindset.

Entrepreneurs have the ability and the power to be flexible and employees do not.

Let's revisit the Bill Gates example. Bill Gates the entrepreneur had the power and flexibility to change the direction of Microsoft once he realized that he was wrong about the internet. The only reason why he could be flexible is because he owned the company. Employees don't have that type of power to be flexible.

If they want to remain employed that have to do what their employer tells them to do. Case in point, there were probably a few employees who felt that Bill Gates was completely wrong about the internet, but they couldn't do anything about it because they lacked the power to override Bill Gates' decision.

Entrepreneurs are revolutionary and innovative and think outside of the box while employees think "inside of the box".

Did you know that most entrepreneurs think of ways to revolutionize the way things are done? Think about it, Jeff Bezos revolutionized the way that a book is read with the invention of the Kindle and Steve Jobs revolutionized the way a phone is used with the creation of the IPhone.

What about Bill Gates and his revolutionary thinking for the Windows operating system? All three of these guys revolutionized industries simply because they thought "outside of the box". Employees are more focused on conformity and thinking "inside the box" because they do not own the box

Entrepreneurs are value focused while employees are time focused.

Entrepreneurs focus on creating value for people because they know that the more value that they create the more likely it is that they will make money. Creating value is simply offering the marketplace solutions to everyday problems or making life much simpler and easy for others.

Employees are so focused on how much time they are dedicating to a job or task. This is why you will hear them say things like "I worked a lot of overtime this week" or "I worked 70 hours this week." They measure value by the amount of time they put into something.

Employees complain about the resources they are lacking. Entrepreneurs utilize the resources that they have and start a business.

You hear people complain about their jobs all the time. "My job doesn't have this", "My job doesn't have that", "If my job had this, I would be able to do that". Employees let their perceived lack of resources stifle their resourcefulness while entrepreneurs are resourceful and will use what they have to get what they want.

They know that the perfect time to start a business is right now, not when you have X amount of dollars, X amount of free time or when "everything is just right". They have the mindset of "no guts no glory" and echo the belief of that famous Nike commercial that implores us to "Just Do It". Regardless if it's perceived to be the right time to start a business by others, entrepreneurs will proceed anyway and hang their shingle on the door.

In concluding this topic, we have thoroughly analyzed the mindset of the employee versus the mindset of the entrepreneur and you should now have a clear understanding of the differences and the ways of how they both think and act. It is very important for you to have this understanding because if you enter into the entrepreneurial world with an employee's mentality and mindset you will be ill-prepared and you will get slaughtered. You will be like that helpless dog who foolishly decides to do battle with a porcupine only to discover that little bastard has quills that are as sharp as needles.

You must remember that you have been conditioned and brainwashed by a system that was designed by others to make them richer while you settle for the crumbs from their table. A job is nothing more than a 19th and

20th century industrial age concept created by the aptly named "robber barons" like John D. Rockefeller who controlled a great portion of the oil industry through his company Standard Oil.

There was also Andrew Carnegie who controlled a great portion of the steel and railroad industries, Cornelius Vanderbilt railroads and shipping, Charles Crocker(railroads),Daniel Drew (finance),James Buchanan Duke (tobacco),James Fisk (finance),Andrew Mellon(finance),J. P. Morgan (finance) Henry Ford (the automobile industry)and others.

These robber barons invented the "job concept" because they needed compliant dependent thinking people to work in the industries that they controlled. They were ruthless in their tactics and the business methods that they employed were widely viewed as illegal, immoral, unethical, and corrupt, and they were known for taking every advantage over workers and consumers hence the nickname "robber barons".

As we moved into the 20th and 21st century the harsh practices that were endured by American workers during the beginning of the industrial age somewhat softened for the worker. The worker was now referred to as an employee. The robber barons went underground and became less visible by hiding behind the many corporations and trusts that they created so it would be hard for the people to point their finger directly at them.

Don't be fooled to believe that the game has changed because you now have "benefits", a 401K, a union etc. as an employee. Nothing has really changed, the game has just gotten slicker. You are still being indoctrinated by institutions and the educational system to be compliant, obedient and forced to give the "right answers" so that you will get good grades and a "good job" that pays well.

Remember that I said the game that you are currently trapped in has gotten slicker? Well now that you have gotten your good job with so called "good pay" you willingly give the majority of your earnings back to the same people who are responsible for indoctrinating you as well as employing you by being the ultimate consumer.

Granted, we all have to consume things, but you are the ultimate consumer and you have spiraled out of control with your consumerism. You buy everything and invest in nothing.

That new IPhone 600 just came out? You go buy it even though the IPhone 599 you bought the year before still works fine. The new Ipad just came out? You got to have it. Don't get me wrong I like new gadgets and shiny new objects too, but I know when to draw the line.

As an entrepreneur I know what to do with the profits that my business generates. A great deal of those profits get reinvested back into the business to expand and grow the business so that I can continue to deliver more value to the marketplace which will result in my business making more profits.

Now the reason why you give your hard earned money up so easily is because let's face it you were programmed to, just as you were programmed to be an employee. You are programmed through the constant bombardment of non-stop advertising that contains strong imagery and powerful associations both verbal and non-verbal that consciously and subconsciously seduce you to buy things.

The programming is along these lines. Buy this gadget and you will be cool. Buy this diamond and she will love you. I'm not against the concept of marketing. In fact, when you transition from being an employee to being an entrepreneur you have to know how to effectively market your products and services to the niche that you are targeting or you will quickly be out of business.

What I'm basically trying to show you is how deep you really have to go mentally if you really want to eradicate your employee mindset. Consumerism and your buying habits are a big part of the employee mindset.

You also have to start realizing and understanding that there are two sides of a coin. You need to look at both sides of the coin if you want to be an entrepreneur. In terms of consumerism and the marketplace there is the seller on one side of the coin and there is the buyer on the other side of the coin. The seller is mainly a producer of products and services and the buyer is mainly a consumer of those products and services. You have to become a producer who offers products and services to the marketplace for profit.

In addition, you have to create and develop a system that runs on autopilot 24-7-365 days out of the year that allows your money to work hard for you rather than you work hard for it. You have to make money even while you sleep. That is the essence of being an entrepreneur.

But in order to get to that stage you must first eliminate and bury your employee mindset forever and reduce it to rubble. The next chapter of this book will show you exactly how to do that and also show you how to make that mental transition from being an employee to being an entrepreneur.

Chapter 4 – Changing Your Mindset – The Transition

The toughest part for you in transitioning from the workforce and employee life to that of being an entrepreneur will be undergoing the necessary process of eradicating your employee mentality and mindset and replacing it with the mentality and mindset of an entrepreneur.

This will be no easy task because it's the equivalent of changing your entire DNA. You have to be deprogrammed because you have been systematically programmed and brainwashed in order for you to fit neatly in and be a part of the employee matrix.

To assist you in deprogramming yourself, I will point out the necessary thought patterns and views you must change or adopt in order to reconstruct your DNA and your composition from that of being a person who breathes, thinks and acts like an employee to one who breathes, thinks, acts and executes like an entrepreneur.

Time Does Not = Money

The first thing you have to do is properly look at the concept of time correctly. All of your life you were told that time equals money and it does not. Time equals

Time and you can never get time back unlike money.

For example, you can't go back to the time when you were eight years old or get the time back you spent reading this book. It's impossible. That time can never be recovered and is spent forever.

Now for money you can easily get it back. For example, you can make a bad investment which results in a loss of money, but you can get that money back. Depending on the amount of money that you lost, you can make or earn that money back in a few weeks, a few months or it may even take you a few years but still you can get it back. So if you can get money back if you lose it and never get time back then time is infinitely more valuable than money.

As an employee you gave your time away to your employer and they were free to do whatever they wanted with your time. They told you how many hours you would work in a given day, what time you would arrive and depart from work, how long you would perform a given task, the amount of time you had to eat lunch and in some cases the amount of time you had to use the bathroom (can you imagine that?). Your time was absolutely controlled from start to finish. You gave up your time, freedom and control for a paycheck.

As an entrepreneur you have to understand and transition to the mindset that your most valuable asset besides your brain is your time. You must value it and you must be ruthless in managing it because time is precious and it is limited.

The bottom line is from the minute that you were conceived the time clock began ticking on your life. The reality is everyone on the planet earth has an expiration date and yes that includes you. So don't waste your time and avoid the time vampires who try to steal and suck up your time. You must also eradicate the foolish belief that time equals money.

Now does that mean that there isn't a relationship between time and money? Let me make this clear, there is absolutely a relationship between time and money when it comes to business, but it's straight forward in that how you spend and allocate your time as an entrepreneur will play a significant role in determining how much money you will make if any.

Allocate your time effectively, efficiently, and judiciously and it should result in profits if you are offering a commercially viable product or service. Allocate it inefficiently or ineffectively, and it will be the death of your entrepreneurial pursuit.

Being Financially Literate and Having a Financial Education is a Must

You have to become financially literate if you truly intend on being successful as an entrepreneur. Financial literacy involves the ability to use knowledge and skills to effectively manage financial resources. It is also the ability to understand how money works in the real world.

The majority of people are financially illiterate because mainly they do not teach financial literacy in school and when they do teach it most of time you are financially mis-educated. For example, you are not taught the true definition of what an asset or a liability is. In fact, at the college I attended I was taught by a particular instructor who shall remain nameless that a house, car and boat were assets when they were in fact liabilities.

To simply and to easily explain what assets and liabilities are, I am going to give you their definitions as explained in the book Rich Dad Poor Dad by Robert Kiyosaki. "An asset puts money in your pocket while a liability takes money out of your pocket". A house that you own or live in is a liability because there are no revenues associated with it only expenses like a mortgage, property taxes, utilities, insurance etc., all which come out of your pocket.

Now on the other hand, if that same exact house or another one that you own generated revenue in the form of rental income and that income exceeded the monthly incurred expenses then that house becomes an asset, because it is putting money into your pocket and you have a positive cash flow from it.

As an entrepreneur it is essential that you invest your money into income producing assets. Also equally as important is being able to identify and recognize when an asset turns into a liability.

Financial literacy also entails learning the language of business which involves law and accounting. When starting a business you have to learn how to record and track all of your income and expenses relating to that business or hire someone who knows how. The recording and tracking of income and expenses will allow you to measure the profitability of your business.

Furthermore, you should also understand the basics of the three major financial statements and their purpose. The three major financial statements are the balance sheet, the income statement, and the cash flow statement. Each statement tells a different part of the story about a business's financial condition.

Let's briefly review the three major financial statements.

Income Statement

The income statement shows all the income and expenses for a business for a specific time period. The income statement will show you whether your business has made a profit or has incurred a loss which is why income statements are also known as statements of profit and loss or P & L's.

If your business's income statement shows that your income is greater than your expenses you have a net profit. However, if it shows that your expenses are greater than your income you have a net loss.

Balance Sheet

The balance sheet is a financial statement that lists the assets, liabilities and equity of a business at a specific point in time. You can look at a balance sheet to determine the net worth of a business. The way that you determine the net worth of a business is by subtracting the total liabilities from the total assets.

Accounting is based on a double entry system which simply means that for every entry into a business's books there has to be an opposite and equal entry. This results in the net effect of the entries equaling zero and the book being balanced. Hence, the name "balance sheet". Proof of your books being balanced is when your assets equal your liabilities plus your equity.

Statement of Cash Flows

The statement of cash flows also known as the cash flow statement shows the inflow of revenue versus the outflow of expenses from operating, investing and financing activities of a business during a specific period of time. The cash flow statement enables you to analyze whether a business has enough cash flowing to pay its bills. A business can actually be profitable on paper but can fail from a lack of cash flow.

That's why they say "Cash(Flow) is King" because cash is the lifeblood of any business and without it a business will surely die.

A big part of being financially literate is being able to determine if the money that you have invested in your business or endeavor is yielding a return. This is known as return on investment or ROI for short. ROI is equal to the amount of income that you received from an investment divided by the total amount of cash invested.

So say for instance that you have invested $200 in a product and that product made you $50. Your return on investment (ROI) would be 25% and it is calculated the following way:

$$\frac{(\$250 - \$200)}{\$200} = .25 \text{ or } 25\%$$

Break even analysis is another important concept and calculation you must know and understand before you begin investing money in the marketing of your products or services as an entrepreneur. A break even analysis is used to determine how much sales volume your business needs to cover your cost of doing business.

Once you perform a break even analysis it will help you determine whether you priced your product or service correctly and whether or not it is economically feasible for you to go forward with bringing a product or service to the marketplace. Here's the formula that you would use to determine your break-even point in units.

Break-Even In Units

$$\frac{\text{Fixed Costs}}{\text{Selling Price - Variable Costs}}$$

Here's an example that will help you understand and calculate a break-even point. Let's say you were selling boxes of exotic sea shells on your website. It costs you $25 to purchase each box of exotic sea shells wholesale (this represents your variable costs) and you retail them for $60. Your marketing budget is $7,000 for the year which represents your fixed costs. You will need to sell 200 units to break-even. Here's that calculation:

$$\frac{\$7,000}{\$60 - \$25} = \textbf{200 units or boxes of exotic sea shells}$$

Now of course the whole object of investing in any endeavor is to make a profit not just to break even. So as an entrepreneur you have to ask yourself the following question when you have determined your break-even point. Can you easily surpass your break-even amount and be profitable?

If the answer is yes then great, but if you can't see your business surpassing your break-even point by a great deal then you should either reduce your marketing costs or increase your selling price which will have the simultaneous effect of increasing the profit that you make per exotic sea shell box, and lowering the amount of units you need to sell to break-even.

Don't be overwhelmed by this stuff that I am teaching you, it is really quite simple. It's not like you have to become a financial wizard overnight, but it is quite necessary to know the basics before you start out on your journey as an entrepreneur. As an employee depending upon what field your job is in there wasn't a need for you to know this type of information.

The system was already set up for you, all you had to do was show up to work and do your particular job and your employer handled the rest. Your employer took care of the nuances of running a business such as establishing the legal entity of the business, the accounting system, staffing, the marketing and sales etc.

As an entrepreneur you are now responsible for handling these various tasks and nuances. Of course when you are starting out small it is really not that complex. Some of the important things that you will be doing are choosing the legal business structure of your business and keeping the books (either doing them yourself using some sort of accounting software like QuickBooks or hiring a bookkeeper to handle the task).

When choosing a legal business structure in which to operate your business out of it is important for you to be familiar with and understand the various entities that exist and how each one affects the future tax liability of your business. It is also imperative that you understand which business structure affords the best protection in terms of liability. This is why a financial education is a must. Although I can't advise you as to what legal business structure to choose for your business, (you should seek the advice of an attorney and an accountant) I can give you a brief overview of the various legal business structures you have to choose from and their tax and liability ramifications.

Sole Proprietorship

A sole proprietorship is simply you doing business as a one person company. There are minimum filing requirements when using this type of business structure unless you are using a trade or fictitious name. In those cases, you must file a "d/b/a" or doing business as with your state, city or locality. The only fees associated with being a sole proprietor is the licensing fees charged by your city or state local government. These fees are nominal.

Sole Proprietorship and Taxes

The income earned by a sole proprietorship is considered income earned by its owner. All income, expenses profits or losses are reported on schedule "C" on your federal income tax return. The income that you earn as a sole proprietor is subject to a self-employment tax.

As an entrepreneur you shouldn't consider yourself to be self employed because you want to escape that whole employee mindset. You want to create a business that employs others. Why would you want to pay a self employment tax when there are tremendous tax incentives and benefits that the government dishes out for those businesses that create jobs and stimulate the economy?

So think of yourself as a business and choose the appropriate business structure that will allow you to gain any tax advantage that you can.

Sole Proprietorship and Liability

There is a big disadvantage in forming your business as a sole proprietorship and that big disadvantage is you have unlimited liability. Unlimited liability means that if a lawsuit was brought against you by someone who purchased your product or service everything that you own personally is at risk. There is nothing personally shielding or protecting your assets. If a judgment was rendered against you, you will likely lose your personal property. The judge will allow the creditor to attack your personal assets like the money that you have in your bank account to satisfy the judgment.

In addition to this, if your business goes bankrupt you must file for personal bankruptcy protection to avoid the business debts.

General Partnership

A general partnership is an entity that is formed with two or more parties. No paperwork needs to be filed to create a partnership. In fact, it can be formed with a simple handshake. However, for your protection it is better to have a partnership agreement that spells out the terms of the partnership.

If there isn't any partnership agreement in place then the partnership is governed by state law. The majority of the states in the U.S. have adopted the Uniform Partnership act (U.P.A.) which consists of a set of rules of how partnerships should act if they don't have a formal agreement.

General Partnership and Taxes

As a general partnership, there are no specialized business tax forms that you will need to file each year. Instead, you will file an "IRS form 1065". This form simply signifies the profits and losses of the partnership. The reason for this is that this type of partnership is considered to be a "flow through entity". In simpler terms, the profits, losses, expenses, etc. "flow-through" to the individual partners rather than the business as a whole.

The partnership will give each partner what is called an IRS form K-1, which informs them of their share of the business profit or loss. After receiving this form, each partner fills out, and attaches, a "Schedule E" to their individual, annual, tax returns.

General Partnership and Liability

A general partnership has no liability protection for partners. In a general partnership, each partner is liable for lawsuits and debts. Regardless of who may have caused the issue, if it was done under the partnership name, all partners are liable.

There is, unfortunately, no protection for this type of partnership. This being said, if you're still going to go into a general partnership with someone, make your choices carefully and wisely.

Limited Partnership

A limited partnership is a form of partnership similar to a general partnership, except that in addition to one or more general partners, there are one or more limited partners. In order to form a limited partnership you must file a Certificate of Limited Partnership with your secretary of state.

In addition you must specifically define who the general partners and the limited partners are in a limited partnership. This is done by filing a limited partnership agreement with your secretary of state.

The limited partnership agreement also spells out in writing the agreement that the partners have among themselves and also lists the ownership interests, profit percentage interest and any special rights of the general partner and limited partners.

The role, of a general partner, is the management of day to day operations, and they control all investment decisions for the business. Limited partners have a much different role than that of the general partners. They have very limited, if any at all, control over management decisions.

Limited Partnership and Taxes

Just like a general partnership, a limited partnership is treated as a "flow through entity" for tax purposes. I must point out to you that in "flow through" entities, the owners pay individual income taxes on all net profits of the business. This is the case whether they receive those net profits or not.

Limited Partnership and Liability

The general partner in a limited partnership has unlimited liability and if a judgment is rendered against the limited partnership and that partnership doesn't have enough assets to cover the claims, the creditor can go after the general partner's personal assets.

Being a general partner in a limited partnership sounds risky doesn't it? Well it is! To minimize this risk as a general partner instead of making yourself the general partner, you may want to create a corporation for the specific purposes of it being the general partner.

Now unlike the general partner a limited partner has no liability beyond what they initially invested in the partnership.

Creditors can't go after limited partners for the debts of that limited partnership.

In addition, limited partners unlike the general partner are not personally liable for acts committed by the general partner unless they participate in management decisions.

Limited Liability Company (LLC)

Limited Liability Companies or LLCs are a fairly new structure introduced to the world of business, in the United States, that is. The concept has been around, for centuries, in countries such as Germany and Europe. Due to the history, in other countries, many formalities have already been created and case laws adopted. However, this is not the case in the United States. LLCs, in the United States, are still in the infancy stage.

The first step in forming an LLC is to file an "Articles of Organization", with the Secretary of State, within the specific state you intend to do business out of. The "Articles of Organization" specifies your organizational structure, business definition, and operational details of your newly created business.

Once you have filed with the state you are now considered to be a legal LLC business entity. You have the option of writing your own Articles of Organization or utilizing the forms available by your Secretary of State which is highly recommended.

As an LLC, you must also designate a "Registered Agent", which is also specified in your "Articles of Organization". A registered agent is the legal person or business, open during business hours, with a legal physical address, designated to receive all legal services, writings, etc, and must reside in the jurisdiction where the LLC is filed – simply put, a physical presence of someone to receive all legal notices for your newly formed LLC.

Since an LLC is made up of its owners, or members, it is important to know who can be a member of an LLC. A member, typically, can be any individual, another LLC, corporation, or even foreign entities. While most states do not dictate who can be a member, it is important to check with your Secretary of State to determine any and all restrictions, prior to forming your LLC.

With an LLC you have a choice between two management structures. An LLC can be "member managed" where all the members (owners) participate in running the business or "manager-managed" where only designated members or managers are given the responsibility to run the business.

LLC and Taxes

An LLC is also treated as a "flow through entity" for tax purposes. For a single member LLC the reporting requirements are basic. All you have to do is attach an IRS form Schedule

C which is a Profit or Loss from a Business to your Form 1040 individual return.

LLC and Liability

A limited liability company provides protection for its members. The members are not liable beyond their contributions to the company. If the LLC is not able to meet its' debts, the members are not liable for these obligations. In addition, if the LLC is sued the members are not personally liable.

Corporation

A corporation is a business entity that carries its own legal status, separate and distinct from its owners. Its' primary advantage is to provide owners with limited liability against business claims. A corporation requires a filing of an articles or "certificate" of incorporation with the state. There are two types of corporations "C" corporations and "S" corporations. An "S" corporation status must be elected.

Corporation and Taxes

A corporation pays taxes on its net income. A "C" corporation files an IRS form 1120. The primary disadvantage of a "C" corporation is double taxation. Profits are taxed first at corporate tax rates and then again at the individual level when owners receive profits from the corporation in the form of dividends.

An "S" corporation is taxed just like a partnership. It files an information IRS form 1120-S and the profits and losses "flow through" to the shareholders. The S corporation sends each shareholder an IRS K-1 which states the shareholder's share of profits or losses.

Corporation and Liability

The big advantage that you gain in forming your business as a corporation is that a corporation provides limited liability for its owners who are referred to as shareholders. The owners are not personally responsible for the debts and liabilities of the business so the creditors can't pursue the owners' personal assets if a judgment was rendered against the corporation.

Limited Liability Partnership (LLP)

A limited liability partnership or LLP operates similar to a limited partnership but it gives each member of the LLP protection from personal liability.

Limited Liability Partnership and Taxes

A limited liability partnership is also considered a flow through entity for tax purposes. Each partner needs to report his share of the company's income or loss on IRS Form 1065 Schedule K.

Limited Liability Partnership and Liability

In general, the partner in a LLP is not responsible for another partner's debts or liabilities resulting from negligence, malpractice or misconduct. LLPs are primarily designed for professions such as doctors, lawyers and accountants.

I know that this seems like a lot for you to consider in terms of choosing a business structure for your business, but it behooves you to know and understand the ramifications of choosing a particular entity. I have only given you a basic overview that's why it is necessary for you to first consult with a lawyer and an accountant before you pick a specific business structure.

I hope that I have made a convincing case as to why you must become financially literate as an entrepreneur. Being financially literate can mean the difference between you making a great deal of money and keeping a significant portion of that money because you understand the tax advantages that a particular business structure offers or not making the money that you should have because you unnecessarily gave a significant chunk of the money that you made away to Uncle Sam because you weren't knowledgeable about the various legal tax loop holes available to you.

There are many books, courses, and seminars available in the marketplace that can assist you in becoming more financially literate. Having said that, in closing this topic, your financial education should never stop as an entrepreneur because the business world is always evolving and changing and it is essential that you stay abreast of these changes because they will impact your business financially.

You now have to become profit and bottom line conscious

As an employee you aren't focused on whether your employer or the company that you work for is making a profit or not or reaching their bottom line numbers unless you have equity in that company. Your only real concern is making sure that you get paid for your services rendered. That's your bottom line and probably the only other concern you have besides that is hoping that the company that you work for is strong and stable so that you can continue to collect your paycheck.

To be a successful entrepreneur you have to transition from this mindset to the mindset of being profit and bottom line conscious. This entails looking at every facet of your business and making sure everything is functioning correctly and is geared towards making a profit. It is essential that you know and understand what your bottom line numbers are.

Some examples of your bottom line numbers include how much does it costs you to acquire a customer, the lifetime value of that customer, the cost of goods sold for each one of your products, your margins, your break-even point in terms of units, your return on investment(ROI) and your net profit. These are some of your bottom line indicators in addition to others that measure the viability of your business. You must always be aware of and specifically understand the metrics of your business.

In your life as an employee you were given certain instructions by others as to what tasks you were to perform and complete to produce a certain outcome, but now as an entrepreneur you have to become that person who develops the strategic plan for your business, create the tasks necessary to execute that plan and then delegate those tasks to others with specific instructions on how they should perform and complete those tasks.

You don't necessarily have to have 9 to 5 employees to complete these tasks. Initially you will probably be outsourcing these tasks to independent contractors or freelancers because it is more cost efficient to do so. There are an abundance of low cost outsourcing options in the United States as well as in places like the Philippines where you can hire a virtual assistant for around $5 an hour. A great place to find workers in the Philippines is at easyoutsource.com.

Since it will be your responsibility to get the most out of people that you hire as an entrepreneur you must become the consummate leader. Everyone who you hire whether that is an employee or a freelancer will be taking their directions and cues from you. You are the general and the captain of the ship which means you must look, think and act the part and you also must exude supreme confidence in what you are doing. You have to remember that you are no longer an employee, you are now a boss who is in charge of getting the most out of others. Embracing this radical change is one of the keys to making a successful transformation.

You must learn how to ruthlessly manage people and profits

In your employee life you were managed and you felt comfortable being managed by others. However, as an entrepreneur and the captain of the ship, you have to learn how to ruthlessly manage people and profits. You need to understand that nobody will care about your business like you do.

If you decide to hire an employee or utilize the services of a freelancer let me make this crystal clear to you. Their only concern is the amount of money that they can extract from you. This is the cold hard truth you must understand. That's why it is essential that you treat your business as if it were a military operation by setting your standards high in terms of accountability, responsibility and what you expect of others who you hire or employ. This will ensure that you get the results that you aim for.

You must keep your emotions out of the equation. When someone is not performing up to expectations, you get rid of them without hesitation. If a freelancer didn't perform a task properly and according to your specifications tell them to fix it and if they balk whack them without mercy. Even if they have already done a great deal of work on a particular project that you gave them. It doesn't matter, don't pay or accept work from them that's not up to par and doesn't adhere to your specifications.

Why should you pay someone for substandard work? You shouldn't and that's why you have to keep your emotions in check and out the equation. It should not matter or be any concern to you that they have a family to feed or they worked very hard on your project and feel that there should be some sort of compensation for doing so. If you become emotionally attached and capitulate to this utter nonsense, you will be left holding the bag, because after all it is *the money out of your pocket* that will be going to waste not theirs.

You have to respect your money and view and treat your dollars with the utmost respect or they will abandon you or die in that fire

pit known as money hell. They will die as a
result of your money sins which in this case
is paying someone for substandard work. You
have to see your dollars as little soldiers
that you send out to war to capture prisoners
and those prisoners are simply more money and
more profits.

You don't want your dollars to die on the
battle field because you failed to properly
deploy them. This is why you must be ruthless
when managing people, your money and profits,
because if you are not ruthless in these
areas, your business will surely encounter a
horrible death. Now of course you want to
avoid this, so to help you out here are some
helpful tips that you need to pay heed to.

1) **The people you hire to do a job are not
your family or your friends.**

The main reason for hiring someone
is to do a job. Productivity and profits
should be the end result of them doing
their job. Nothing else. You didn't hire
them to be your friend or to treat them
like family. I'm not saying this to be an
asshole, but I see so many entrepreneurs
make the fatal mistake of trying and
wanting to be friends or having some type
of familial relationship with the people
that they hire. This inevitably results
in them losing their objectivity and
clouds their judgment, because emotions
come into play.

When someone needs to be criticized, strongly reprimanded or given the ax, there is hesitation because that person is considered a friend. When you allow yourself to fall into this friendship trap with the people that you hire eventually you will get exploited. Your new found friend will take advantage of you because you have a gaping hole in your armor and familiarity breeds contempt.

They will ask you for favors, make excuses, want you to be their counselor or parent, all because you allowed them to become your "friend". This is not what you went into business for. It's time consuming, counter-productive and an enemy to your profits and bottom line.

Let me ask you a question. In your employee life is the CEO, the president or the owner of the company that you work for trying to be your friend? Of course not, Why? It's because it is not conducive to business. Here are some simple words of advice. If you want a friend go buy a dog.

2) **You must reinvest your profits back into the business.**

This is a simple rule of business and reinvesting the profits that your business makes is one of the more practical ways of growing and expanding your business. There is an old adage in business that says "a business that is not growing is a business that is dying". So make sure that you wisely reinvest a majority of your profits back into your business.

The lifestyle of an entrepreneur often gets exaggerated and badly misrepresented by the media who tend to focus on portraying the glamorous side of being an entrepreneur because it makes for a good story. I'm pretty sure that you have seen the images of super successful rich entrepreneurs living opulent lifestyles, traveling the world, enjoying the finer things in life and being adventurous.

But for most entrepreneurs this is a far cry from reality because when you are building a business the aim is not to foolishly use its profits to fund some fantasy lifestyle. On the contrary, smart and wise entrepreneurs are too busy grinding it out by investing those profits into resources that will produce more income.

In fact, in most cases, an entrepreneur will even forego paying himself a salary to meet this objective. In the beginning this is the life that you will face as an entrepreneur.

3) **Speed and launching your product or service is more important than perfectionism.**

So what is the best time for you as an entrepreneur to launch your product, service or business into the marketplace? The answer is that time is now! Not when everything is perfect. Perfectionism is equivalent to paralysis. The most successful entrepreneurs and businesses are the ones that get to the market quickly and out execute the competition. This is why speed is important. You don't have to perfect your product or service before releasing it to the marketplace.

Case in point, most software companies release less than perfect software to the marketplace. The first version of the software usually contains a few bugs that the software manufacturer is aware of or in some cases not aware of. When the software is released to the public, the software maker usually relies on feedback from customers to make the necessary adjustments or modifications to the software. That is why a version 2 is released. This is an ongoing process, that's why there are always subsequent versions of the original version of the software.

Another notable example of a product being less than perfect when released is when Apple released the IPhone 4 and it had an antenna problem. Did Apple know that the IPhone had an antenna problem before releasing the IPhone 4? Maybe, but it didn't stop them from launching the product because they knew that getting it to the marketplace quickly would enable them to capture a significant piece of the marketplace as well as the minds and the imagination of the public.

When customers in droves began to complain about the problem with the antenna, Apple offered them free bumpers to alleviate the problem or $15 dollars in cash. Despite its antenna flaws, the IPhone was a smashing success, which is why speed and getting to the marketplace is more important than perfectionism.

4) **Don't make or accept excuses, because if you do it will weaken you as well as your business.**

Excuses are for losers so don't accept or make them. Everything in your business as an entrepreneur begins and

ends with you. You are 100% accountable
for the state that your business is in
whether that is a good state or a bad
state, a profitable state or a losing
money state. You must own up to the
results that you produce and if you don't
like the results change your strategy or
plan to produce a more favorable outcome.

5) **When you hire people to perform tasks for
your business make sure that you are the
one that is setting the pace and the
deadlines not them.**

As an entrepreneur you will be
responsible for determining the pace for
your business. You have to decide on what
things are done fast, slow or in a
deliberate methodical way. When you hire
someone you have to make sure that you
don't allow them to set the pace and the
timeframe when things are to be done,
because if you allow this to happen
whomever you hire is effectively
controlling the destiny of your business
and you should be the one that is doing
that.

If you have a project that needs to
be completed in less than a week state
that strongly and be adamant about it. If
they can't meet your deadline, get rid of
them and get someone that will. If you
start making concessions you will fail at

accomplishing your goals in a timely manner. You must never hand over the reins of your business to anyone by letting them decide when things will be done.

I don't know whether you will admit to this or not, as an employee more often than not you paced yourself when it came to your work. Am I correct? If you were given a deadline of 1 week to complete a project but you knew that you could finish it in one day didn't you stretch it out for a few more days or out to the entire week?

If you answered that you would have completed it in one day then bravo! You are one of the rare few. However, I know that you know of others who you work with at the job who would have decided to pace themselves and stretch it out for a few more days or out to the entire week.

Heck you probably even know some fellow employees who would ask the boss for more than the 1 week time limit to complete the task even though they know that they could complete it in one day. These are the get over types. People who look to con who's ever in charge, because either they are lazy or simply want to manipulate their employer to allow them to work at their own pace.

As an entrepreneur you can't fall for this con. You have to be steadfast in setting your deadlines and if anyone finds it hard to comply then you must ruthlessly whack them or your productivity and business will suffer.

6) Ruthlessly eliminate non-essential components of your business.

Get rid of products or services that don't work or make you any money. They are a waste of your time and energy and are a drain on cash. Instead you should focus on the products and services that work and that have high margins. Focusing on high margin products and services can make you rich fast. You have to consistently monitor the efficiency of your business and cull when necessary. This will enable you to build a lean mean profitable machine.

Hopefully these tips serve as a guide for you and I hope that I made it crystal clear to you the importance of ruthlessly managing people, money and profits. Now let's continue with your makeover.

You must transition to the mindset that your business is your life and your life is your business because they are

indeed interconnected and intertwined with each other.

Basically, what this means is as an entrepreneur is that you eat, sleep and think the business and there is no such thing as quitting time, maybe physically but never mentally. This is radically different from the mindset of an employee who believes when that clock says 5pm or whenever quitting time is the job is over. The mindset is, there isn't any need to even think about that job until they arrive the next day at work and sit at their desk inside a little Dilbert's cubicle or whatever contraption that houses them.

To make an effective transition to an entrepreneurial mindset you must eradicate this type of thinking. When you are building a business in reality there is little time for anything else if you want to succeed.

As an employee you are part of an overall system, a cog in a machine if you will, that was envisioned and created by your employer or the owner of the company that you work for. As an entrepreneur you now are responsible for the task of creating a system for your business so that it runs efficiently and effectively to produce profits. You shouldn't get scared off or overwhelmed by the prospects of creating a system for your business, because all a system basically is are predetermined procedures and methods of getting things done.

Regardless of how big or small your business will be you must create a system that runs on auto-pilot 24/7. The hallmark of a great business is its systems. For example, we all know that McDonalds doesn't make the greatest hamburgers in the world, but its franchise system is arguably one of the best if not the best business system of all time. That juggernaut of a system is responsible for serving billions of burger and fries to people every day.

Ray Kroc founder of the McDonald's franchise called this system the McDonald's method which is basically a system that explained to the franchisees exactly how things were to be done; How much meat to include in a hamburger, how long to cook that hamburger, how to cut the fries, when to order inventory and even how often to clean the restaurant.

Ray Kroc even launched a training program called (I kid you not) Hamburger University, where franchisees and operators were trained in the scientific methods of running a successful McDonalds.

Likewise, you must create a bona-fide system for every aspect of your business. The systems that you would create for your business can be broken down into the following 3 components.

1) **Marketing**- You must create a marketing system that will enable you to become

visible to the marketplace, attract and acquire new customers and follow up with old customers. This is the "getting business" component of your system and it involves lead generation, direct response marketing and the overall sales process.

As an entrepreneur the type of marketing that you will be primarily using to get customers for your business is called direct response marketing. Direct response marketing is designed to generate an immediate response from consumers. This response can easily be measured and attributed to a specific advertisement that generated the results. Direct response marketing can be delivered through mediums such as direct mail, newspaper ads, print advertising, radio, T.V., telemarketing and the internet.

Once you have elicited a response from prospects through your direct response campaigns you have to have a system in place to capture the responders' information so that you can follow up with them. If you are driving them to your website this is accomplished by having a form on your site that asks them for essentials such as their name and email address. Once they have entered this information into the form and have opted in to receive your email messages, there should be an autoresponder system in place that contains prewritten information that you schedule to be sent out automatically at different intervals via email.

The intended purpose of your sequential email follow up messages is to educate your prospects further about the product or service that you are offering and hopefully as they become more familiar with you and the benefits of what you are offering it will result in sales. Selling is a process and you must have an automated system in place that generate leads, capture and nurture those leads, closes the sale and fulfills the order.

In my book "**How To Market Your Business Online and Offline**" I go into deeper details on how to effectively market your business.

2) **Fulfillment** – Once you have made the sale of your product or service you need to fulfill that order and deliver on those promises that you made during the sales process. You need to create a system for fulfilling the order and this includes shipping the item or making it available for download if you're selling a digital product, or if you're selling a service such as a coaching or mentoring program scheduling the dates and preparing and

delivering the coaching or mentoring materials to your client. This is the "doing the business" component of your system.

3) **Financial and Administration** – As mentioned earlier, there must be a system in place to record, track and analyze the financial aspects of your business. There has to be an accounting system in place that records and tracks such things as revenue, expenses, accounts payable, accounts receivable etc. The administrative part of your system is a process that you institute that dictates how you will screen, hire and evaluate freelancers or employees that you may hire. Both the financial and administrative parts of your system represent the "running the business" component of your system.

Chapter 5-Your Money Blueprint and Changing The Way You Think About Money

Everyone has a view or opinion about money. Believe it or not most of your views and beliefs about money were heavily influenced by your parents and what they thought about money. They were essentially your first teachers on the subject. Now the questions that you have to ask yourself are, were the lessons that you learned from them about money helpful or detrimental? This is very important because the lessons that you learned about money are deeply ingrained in you and help to form what is known as your money blueprint.

Your money blueprint is basically your core beliefs about money and these core beliefs are one of the components that will determine whether you embrace the idea of making a lot of money or reject it because you are repulsed by that notion. You may not even be consciously aware that you are repulsed by the idea of making a lot of money, but if you grew up in an environment where you constantly heard such things as "rich people are greedy", "money doesn't grow on trees" and other similar expressions, these beliefs are probably and unfortunately embedded in your subconscious mind.

Now you are probably thinking what does this have to do with entrepreneurship? Well for starters if you have negative beliefs about money how can you expect to make any as an online entrepreneur? And if you are fortunate and are able to make some money your negative beliefs will more than likely have you limiting the amount of money that you can make or sabotaging it entirely because you have the belief that "money is the root of all evil" and "rich people are greedy".

In addition to this, your money blueprint will also be reflective of how low or high your financial thermostat is set at. What I mean by your financial thermostat is, are you programmed to set low financial goals or high financial goals for your online business? Your money blueprint may dictate that you are completely comfortable and satisfied with building a $100,000 company or it may dictate that you are completely comfortable and satisfied with building a 10 million dollar company or a multibillion dollar online company like Facebook or Twitter. Only you can answer that.

Personally, my financial thermostat is set to the multibillion dollar range as far as building and growing an online business is concerned. You know why? It's because I am not afraid of big numbers and I believe in thinking big. Thinking big or thinking small is a matter of choice and the choice that you make will be based on your money blueprint and where your financial thermostat is set at. If you don't like your present money blueprint or where your financial thermostat is set at, change it. You change it by first honestly assessing your beliefs about money and then identifying those beliefs that are negative or hinder you and feverishly work to eliminate them from your belief system.

If your problem is that you don't think big enough, then you have self-limiting beliefs that are holding you back that you must completely obliterate in order to transform yourself into a person who thinks and acts big. It is not enough to just change from an employee mindset to the mindset of an entrepreneur, you have to analyze and look at your entire mindset and make sure that there is nothing standing in your way or stopping you from achieving unlimited success.

I know that there might be some challenges for you as you go forward and move towards tweaking, correcting or creating an entirely new money blueprint for yourself, so to assist you I've written a detailed book that is solely dedicated to this topic entitled **Money Blueprint: The Secrets to Creating Instant Wealth.** In addition, I've also written another valuable book that will assist you in developing an indomitable mindset entitled **The Killer Instinct: How to Master It and Achieve Anything That You Want.**

Chapter 6 - Why Be An Online Entrepreneur?

Obviously you bought this book because of the promise of its title which is to show you how to transform yourself from an employee to an online entrepreneur, but the question begs why online entrepreneurism? The answer is, there are many distinct advantages in starting a business online.

1) **Low startup and overhead costs** - The start-up costs are minimal when compared to the cost of starting a brick and mortar business. For less than $500 you can basically get a website and blog built and you are in business. Also you can run and operate an online business from your home virtually eliminating most traditional offline business overhead costs like renting an office space, insurance, office equipment etc.

2) **You can conduct business worldwide** - You can basically sell products or services to anybody in any country as long as they have access to the internet. Your market and targeted audience isn't limited by a physical location.

3) **Operate 24/7** - You are never closed for business and it doesn't matter if it's 2 a.m. or 2 p.m. your website will operate 24 hours, 7 days a week earning you money while you're asleep.

4) **Unlimited potential income** – Unlike a 9-5 job where there is a cap on wages and the amount of income you make is determined by the amount of hours that you work there is no limit to how much money you can earn from an online business.

5) **Scalability** – Depending on the ecommerce business model chosen, online businesses are easy scalable. Scaling is the ability to grow a business at a rapid or compound rate with minimal or no increase in operating costs.

6) **Freedom and flexibility** – Having an online business affords you the freedom and flexibility to work from anywhere. You can work from home, an office, a coffee shop or at anyplace anywhere in the world as long as you have an internet connection.

In addition to these distinct advantages, the following statistics bear witness to the fact that there is no better time than right now to be an online entrepreneur and start an online business.

- According to Forrester Research, online spending in the United States alone is projected to be $262 Billion in 2013. In 2017 it's forecasted to be $370 Billion.

- According to eMarketer, Business to Consumer (B2C) worldwide ecommerce sales is forecasted to be 1.298 trillion dollars in 2013.
- Almost 250 million searches for products and businesses are performed per day on Google alone.
- Every year, more than 100 million Americans purchase goods from the online retail marketplace.

Despite the many advantages that starting an online business has to offer and the glowing statistics just mentioned, there are some harsh realities that I must point out so that you don't falsely get the impression that every aspiring entrepreneur who decides to start an online business experiences success. In fact, the reality is the failure rate is quite high not just for online entrepreneurs, but for entrepreneurs in general. According to the Small Business Administration (SBA) 50% of all businesses fail in the first year and 95% of them fail in the next 5 years.

Now this doesn't mean that you will personally fail, what it means is that most people who make that journey will. Keep in mind that most successful entrepreneurs have failed the first time around only to be successful at a later date simply because they didn't quit. They realize that failure is sometimes part of the process before eventually succeeding. However, having said that there are specific reasons why a lot of aspiring entrepreneurs fail at their goal of having a successful online business. Here are some of them.

1) **They start a business for all the wrong reasons** – Being passionate about something can be a great thing however, just because you are passionate about something doesn't necessarily mean that you should turn what you're passionate about into a business. A lot of aspiring entrepreneurs fall into this trap mainly because they get brainwashed by the "passion gurus". You know exactly the gurus I'm talking about, the ones that preach to you to "follow your passion and the money will follow".

   The harsh reality is that the money and the profits will only follow if the marketplace is willing to purchase what you have to offer. The marketplace could care less about your passion. I'm passionate about basketball does that mean I should build a website and sell basketballs? Of course not! Sadly that's what some people do, they dive head first into starting a business without really thinking it through or doing any market research to determine if in fact a strong enough market exists to build a sustainable business based on their passion.

Bottom line, people start businesses for all the wrong reasons. For example, they may start a business to spend time with their family or as a popular book suggests to work "the 4 hour work week" which in itself is absurd. The truth of the matter with entrepreneurship is you will work endless hours, have little time for family or friends and if you plan on succeeding you will be totally focused on your business.

Other wrong reasons for starting a business include:
- Starting a business to get rich quick.
- Starting a business because it's the in thing to do.
- Starting a business because you hate your boss.

2) **They fail to differentiate** - Most businesses fail because they don't differentiate themselves or their products and services from the competition and existing solutions in the marketplace. If you want to succeed you must be unique and set yourself apart from the pack. You must build your business on things that are hard to duplicate and are proprietary in nature. This will give you a competitive advantage in the marketplace. Lack of a

competitive advantage in the marketplace will be fatal to any business.

3) **They lack capital**- Most businesses fail because they have insufficient operating funds. Many entrepreneurs make the fatal mistake of underestimating how much money is needed to start, operate and stay in business. In order to avoid failure because of the lack of funds, an entrepreneur must make sure that they raise or borrow enough funds that will enable them to run their business in an effective manner. They also should make allowances for the unexpected because running a business that has no margin for error is a disaster waiting to happen.

4) **They have poor marketing or no marketing at all**- Marketing is the lifeblood of any business. It is the fuel that produces the leads and prospects for a business. Prospects turn into customers and customers sustain a business and enables it to thrive. A business will absolutely fail if its marketing is ineffective and inefficient and it doesn't have a chance if there is no marketing at all. It is only through marketing that your potential customers will hear about your business and your products or services. Entrepreneurs who poorly market their business or who don't market their business at all inevitably fail.

5) **They don't know how to run a business**– Aspiring entrepreneurs often fail at business simply because they don't have a clue on how to run a business. They know very little about marketing, how to write sales copy, how to implement systems that will enable the business to run on autopilot, how to build an infrastructure that will support the business and so on.

Before you jump into starting your online business, you should prepare yourself by reading books on the topics I've just mentioned. Also you should read books authored by successful entrepreneurs who have already been there and done that in terms of what you're looking to accomplish as an entrepreneur. A really good book along those lines is Delivering Happiness: A Path to Profits, Passion, and Purpose by Zappos.com founder Tony Hsieh.

6) **They go at it alone** – There are many tasks involved in running a business so it's virtually impossible to do everything on your own and be efficient and optimally productive. Entrepreneurs who try to do everything by themselves usually fail because they are not using their time in the correct manner. They spend their valuable time focusing on mundane and minor tasks that they could

easily outsource to someone else which will allow them to focus on executing the main tasks which are important to a business like marketing and bringing in the revenue.

You can never really grow a business by yourself fast without using leverage. Leverage involves using other people's talent, time and money to further your business. Smart and successful entrepreneurs prefer building a winning team and relying on the strength of that team to build a successful business.

7) **They try building a business around products and services that there isn't enough demand for or doesn't generate repeat business.**

Before launching a product or service it is imperative that you do the appropriate research to determine whether or not there is a strong enough market or demand for what you intend to sell. For example, before I got into the business of audio books I did my due diligence in terms of researching the market. I knew that there was a market for audio books but before diving into the business head first I had to determine the size of the market, who the major players were in terms of distribution and if there was enough repeat business to build a sustainable business.

The information that I gathered that aided me and strongly encouraged me to proceed forward with this venture was the following. The audio book business was a 2 billion dollar a year industry, the major players in terms of distribution were some heavy hitters and these heavy hitters included Amazon, Audible and Apple and the average audio book customer purchased 17 audio books annually which signified repeat customers. This led me to the conclusion that I would be able to build a sustainable business over the long term.

Entrepreneurs who neglect to do this basic type of research before launching a business unnecessarily find themselves in trouble and before long their out of business simply because they didn't find out first it there was a strong enough market for what there were trying to sell, the size of that market and the ability to create a sustainable business over the long term.

8) **They have a poor pricing strategy** – Entrepreneurs who have poor pricing strategies for their product and services go out of business because the economics dictate that they should. As an

entrepreneur you have to make sure you price your products and services at a level that will ensure that you are profitable. A business that doesn't make a profit is a problem and will soon be out of business. Nobody gets into business to lose money and a business that consistently loses money is nothing more than an expensive hobby.

Some entrepreneurs have a problem extracting premium prices for their products and services simply because they engage in selling products and services that are considered to be commodities or they are in a commoditized business. If you are in a commoditized business and are selling a commoditized product or service, that means that there are a ton of people in the marketplace that are selling exactly what you are selling. There is nothing to distinguish you from your competition. You lack uniqueness.

So people will only buy from you based on your price. The problem with that is there is always someone who is willing to sell what you are selling cheaper. So where does that leave you as an entrepreneur? In my estimation it puts you and your business in a very vulnerable position.
You're vulnerable because your competitors will slash their prices to

compete with you with little regard to
how it will even affect their profits.
Since consumers are price conscious when
it comes to commoditized products or
services you have no choice but to slash
your prices to match your competition.
This price slashing spiral goes on and on
until you can't do it any longer, throw
in the towel or eventually go out of
business.

Now there are ways to avoid this pitfall
and here's what I strongly suggest when
deciding what products and services to
sell in your online business. You should
either create your own proprietary
product or service or add a proprietary
aspect to an existing product or service
or do both. When you create a proprietary
product or service you can charge a
premium price because what you are
offering is truly unique and you have
differentiated yourself from your
competition. Now what I mean by adding a
proprietary aspect to an existing product
or service is you can actually take
something that is being sold in the
marketplace by others as well as yourself
and that is considered to be a commodity
and add something proprietary to it to
make it unique and stand out from the
pack.

For example, Zappos.com sells shoes which are a commodity. However, to differentiate themselves from their competitors Zappos created a proprietary method for selling shoes and doing business. First of all they have superior customer service and they have an unheard of 365 day return policy that is unmatched. You can buy shoes from them and if you are dissatisfied with your purchase you have up to a year to return them.

To make their offer even more you unique they also have a two-way free shipping policy. When a customer orders from them they ship the shoes out free and if the customer wants to return their shoes, Zappos will also pay to have the shoes picked up. By simply creating a proprietary way of selling shoes and doing business Zappos has built a successful company and sell over a billion dollars worth of shoes annually.

9) **They lack execution** - It isn't enough that you have an idea or a strategic plan because it's only a start. To bring your ideas into fruition or to put your plan in motion to accomplish your objectives and goals you have to execute. Many entrepreneurs fail at business because they don't know how to execute. The bottom line is, if you want a specific

outcome you must take specific actions. This is what execution is all about.

As you can clearly see there are many advantages, challenges, obstacles and potential pitfalls in starting an online business, but hopefully this particular chapter has given you some valuable insight as well as guidance that will help you as you proceed forward in starting, building and growing your online business.

Chapter 7 – Online Business Essentials

Before we discuss the various online business models in which you can adopt and create your business from, I would like to go over the online business essentials that anyone who is starting a business should be familiar with. Now I don't know what your particular level of knowledge is when it comes to this area so this chapter will either enlightened you if you are not familiar with its contents, or serve as a review for you if you are already familiar with the fundamentals and essentials elements that are needed to start any type of online business.

Business Name

Choosing a name for your business is important because it identifies to the public and signifies in most cases what you do. It is your business's identity and your brand so you must choose a name that serves you well, is unique and differentiates your business from other businesses and brands in the marketplace. There are also other considerations to take into account as well. Here are some tips and suggestions that you should consider when choosing a name for your business.

Try to imagine how the potential name will look or sound – Visualize how it would look on business cards, logos, on advertisements and your website. Does it look good? Is it snappy or catchy enough? Can it be easily remembered? Does it distinguish you from your competitors? How does it sound when you say it or when you visualize others saying it? Is it easy to pronounce? These are some of the things that you have to consider when deciding on a name for your business.

Also you want to choose a name that works well on the Web since this is an online business. Once you have come up with a name that you like, you want to conduct a domain name search. A domain name search will determine whether you can set up a website that has a web address or domain name exactly as the name of your business. You can perform a quick domain search through the WHOIS database located at http://www.whois.net.

If it is determined that the name has already been claimed by someone you might want to reconsider the name of your business. However, if the name is that important to you, you can also obtain the contact information of the person or the company that owns it from the WHOIS database, contact them and offer to buy the domain name from them. Another thing that you want to take into account in addition to the availability of the domain name is whether your business's name is available on social media sites like Facebook, Twitter or Google+ to ensure that no other businesses or brands are operating in the social networking world with the same or similar name.

Domain Name

We've already discussed some of the important aspects of a domain name. Your domain name along with your website's URL address is the only way that people would be able to access your site online and without a domain name obviously you won't be able to have an online business that you completely control. I can't stress enough the importance of having the same domain name as your business name. In this day and age people are already programmed with the notion that if they want to find your business's website all they would have to know is your business's name and put the prefix www. before it and .com at the end of it and they will be able to access your site on the internet.

So imagine if someone else had a domain name with the same name as your business and you had an entirely different domain name. You begin to spend your money on marketing and advertising highlighting the products that you have to offer, as well as the name of your business for branding purposes. It is a known fact that the majority of people don't retain everything that they hear, see or read in an advertisement.

For example, maybe they remember your product or service and the name of your business, but they forget your business's telephone number or website address. In the case of the latter, as I said previously if they remember the name of your business they will instantly assume that all they would have to do is add the www. prefix before it and the extension .com after it and they will be able to reach your site and buy what you have to offer.

Let's say that 50% of the people that you reach do this, wouldn't it be a disaster for you if they go to the other website that has the domain name as your business assuming that it was yours? Furthermore, what if that particular website was selling the same exact products that you were selling and as a result of your marketing they were making sales instead of you? You would be foolishly aiding and abetting the competition to your own detriment and demise simply because you made the poor decision to name your business before securing the domain name for it or the domain name wasn't available and you simply ignored it.

Another huge mistake that people make when choosing a domain name is that they only purchase the .com extension for their site. It is in your best interests to also purchase the other major extensions like .org, .net, .co and .info to ensure that no one else purchases them with the intent to nefariously capitalize off of your brand's name. My last and final thoughts on the subject of domain names: You should never choose a hyphenated domain name for your business because it is so easy for people to forget to type or remember the hyphen.

Website

The website that you create will of course be determined by what type of online business that you're in and the type of products and services that you are offering. There are several ways that you can go about creating a website for your online business. You can build it yourself if you have knowledge of coding, or if you have limited knowledge of coding or no knowledge of coding what so ever you can use a software solution like Dreamweaver to assist you. You can also outsource the task of building your website to a competent website designer who has the knowledge and experience with the type of website you are trying to build as well as some familiarity with the niche you are targeting.

Also your website designer must be familiar with search engine optimization to ensure that the website that you are building is both user and search engine friendly. Here are some other things that you should consider when building a website for your online business.

1) **Your web audience** – Basically these are the potential customers that you are

trying to attract and they must influence every aspect and decision when it comes to the design of your website. When designing your website you want to make sure that it is geared towards an excellent user experience, is easy to navigate and is free of clutter.

2) **Your website's content** – You want to make sure that the content that you put on your website is relevant to your audience and has a specific purpose. For example, maybe your content is designed to position you or your business as an authority in a particular niche, or maybe it is designed to explicitly to describe the products and services that you have to offer.

Regardless of the purpose, you have to make sure that your content is search engine optimized so that when potential customers perform a search query looking for particular products or services on the line of what you have to offer, your website is visible and ranks high in the search engines for its main keywords.

3) **Scalability** – Your website may start off as small with only a few web pages, but you want to make sure that your site is built with growth in mind. The design should be flexible and allow you to add additional web pages as needed.

4) **Tracking** – You want to be able to track, measure and analyze everything that happens on your website. This is referred to as your website metrics. Your website's metrics will include the following: The amount of visitors that you receive at your website, the most popular landing pages, the bounce rate which is basically how long your website's visitors stay on your site and your conversion rate which is a measurement of how many visitors your website is receiving and how many of those visitors are converting to customers. The formula to calculate your conversion rate is as follows:

# of sales/# of visitors X 100 = The visitor to customer conversion rate

So if you received a total of 5,000 visitors for the month at your website and 170 of those visitors became customers, then your visitor to customer conversion rate is 3.4%. Analyzing your website's metrics is basically the only way that you will be able to determine what's working or not working on your website and the overall effectiveness of your marketing and advertising campaigns. Google offers a free tool and service called Google Analytics that will enable you to track and measure the performance of your website.

Web Hosting

Web hosting is essential because without it your website couldn't be seen on the internet. The way that web hosting works is a web hosting company or service allocates space on their servers for their customer's websites, which enables these websites to be seen and have a presence on the internet. The servers are connected to the internet around the clock which allows a website to be available 24/7. The web hosting company allows a certain amount of bandwidth for each and every site that they host. The amount of bandwidth that a site is allowed depends on the particular web hosting plan that is chosen.

When choosing a web hosting company for your online business there are many factors that you have to take into consideration. Here are a few of those factors.

- **Storage space** – You have to make sure the web hosting company that you are considering offers an adequate amount of storage space, because you really can never predict how much storage space you might need. Your website may start off small requiring very little storage space, but as you grow more maybe needed. If that turns out to be the case you want to make sure that you are able to upgrade to the capacity of storage space that you need.

- **Bandwidth** – You also want to make sure that the hosting company that you are considering offers a suitable amount of bandwidth. The amount of bandwidth is important because it determines how much traffic your website will be able to handle at a given time. If you use your allotment of bandwidth your website will be shut down until you upgrade your bandwidth capabilities. Usually most web hosting companies advertise that they offer an "unlimited amount of bandwidth", but if you carefully read the fine print you will discover that this is not the case.

- **Reliability** – Choosing a web hosting service that is reliable is of utmost importance to your online business. You can assess a web hosting company's reliability by asking them about their guaranteed uptime percentages for each plan that they provide. If their guaranteed uptime percentage is below 98% in my opinion they are not a reliable web hosting company. You are running a business and can ill-afford for your website to be down frequently or for any extended period of time. Frequent or extended periods of downtime affect your traffic levels, your income, and your business's credibility.

- **Security** – The web hosting company that you are considering must offer strong security to safeguard your valuable information and data. They should offer 128 bit SSL certificate encryption for all data transfers and have file transfer security measures such as Secure File Transfer Protocol (SFTP).

- **Supported web programming languages** – It's best to choose a web hosting service that supports multiple web programming languages like Ruby, Perl and PHP because it gives you flexibility and the option of changing the web programming of your site without too much of a hassle if you decide to go in another direction.

- **Customer service** – The reality is that issues will come up from time to time regarding your website and you want to be able to call your web hosting service provider no matter what time of the day it is to resolve any issues that arise. So when choosing your web hosting provider make sure that they offer 24 hours customer service and technical support.

Autoresponder System

An autoresponder system is another one of those online business essentials that you must have in your arsenal. I've just went over it somewhat, but this tool is such of an importance that I feel that it is absolutely necessary to review it again and go into further detail.

An autoresponder system allows you to capture your website's visitor's information like their name and email address via a form on your website. The form is simply a snippet of HTML code that you insert on the web page where you want to place your form. You have to first design the form and the autoresponder service that you sign up with provides you with ready-made templates that you can edit and customize to create your own form.

When your website's visitors fill out this form they will automatically start receiving pre-written email messages from you at different intervals that you schedule. The autoresponder service that you sign up with handles the sending of the emails as well as the creation and maintenance of the database which contains the information of all of the people who filled out the form on your website and opted in to receive your email messages.

In order to get your website visitors to fill out your form and opt in to receive email messages from you, you have to entice them by offering them something "free" such as a free report, free e-course, free audio or video presentation etc. Normally this information that you give away for free contains content that is designed to educate your prospects further about your products and services with the intention of getting the sale. People don't usually buy from you the first time that they visit your site, that's why it is extremely important and necessary for you to get their information so that you can follow up with them.

After receiving a few correspondences from you via email they become familiar with you and your business. They then gain the confidence that is needed to make a purchase. The two most popular autoresponder services that you can choose from are AWeber located on the web at http://www.aweber.com and Get Response located at http://www.getresponse.com.

A Way to Accept Payments

Of course you are in the business of making money so you have to be able to process payments on your website. There are a plethora of options that you can choose from to accomplish this, however the best option based on my personal experience is PayPal. PayPal allows you to create payment buttons for the items that you are selling on your website. These payment buttons can be edited and customized to suit your specific needs. PayPal even allows you to accept recurring subscription payments from your customers.

The subscription payment feature is perfect if you plan on a creating a membership site or if you have some type of consulting service where you charge a monthly fee. PayPal automatically collects the subscription payment from your customers for you. PayPal also offers a free shopping cart system which allows your customers to browse your entire selection of products, purchase multiple items per order and view a list of their items in their shopping cart before purchasing.

Even if you decide to use a full featured shopping cart from another provider, PayPal offers a seamless integration that will have you up and running in no time. Before purchasing a shopping cart from another provider check to see if it's compatible with PayPal. PayPal offers a list of shopping cart providers on their website who are compatible with PayPal.

PayPal is free to join and to receive credit card payments on your website you have to sign up for a business premier or merchant account and also have a checking account which you must verify and confirm. The way that the PayPal confirmation process works is when you register your checking account with PayPal they make two small deposits into your checking account. You must then find out from your bank or check your bank statement to verify the amounts that were deposited. Once you have correctly verified those amounts with PayPal, your PayPal account becomes confirmed. This confirmation process serves as a security measure for PayPal. It establishes that you are the owner of the checking account or you have authorization to do business with it.

PayPal charges you a fee to receive money. They charge 2.9% of the total amount received for each transaction plus a .30 cent transaction fee. There are three ways to access your money from your PayPal account. You can transfer it directly into your checking account associated with PayPal which is free, you can withdraw it using a PayPal debit card with the obvious fees associated with choosing that option or you can request a check from PayPal for the balance in your account which costs $1.50.

Copywriting Skills

What is copywriting and why is it essential to your online business? Copywriting is the art and science of strategically using words to persuade and influence the audience that you are targeting to take a specific action like making a purchase or signing up for something that you have to offer.

On your website and in your correspondences with your prospects and customers you will be using the written word whether it is in the form of text, audio or video to get into their psyche with the goal of hitting the right combination of emotional triggers that will produce the action or results that you want. This is the essence of copywriting and obviously this requires having a certain amount of skill and understanding of not only how to tell a story, but how to magically use words that sell. This is why great copywriters get paid handsomely, because they possess this valuable and sort after skill and have a proven track record for getting results for their clients that shows up in the cash register.

Now, can you learn how to be a great copywriter specifically for your online business? Of course you can, but you have to be willing to work at it by studying, learning, and mastering the fundamentals of this craft. You can speed up your learning curve by studying the great copywriters like Dan Kennedy or the late Gary Halbert as well as others. Personally, I do all of the copywriting for my business, because I am great at it myself.

If you want to learn the fundamentals of great copywriting and how to effectively sell your products and services online read my book entitled: **How To Sell Any Product Online: Secrets of The Killer Sales Letter.**

Search Engine Optimization (SEO)

There is no way of getting around this online business essential. If you want your website to be found by others throughout the world it must be search engine optimized. So what exactly is search engine optimization or SEO for short? Search engine optimization is the process and science of making sure that a website is relevant to the search engines so that it is able to gain visibility by ranking high for its main keywords and keyword phrases.

This process involves on-page optimization and off-page optimization. On-page optimization involves working on the elements on your website that directly influences and impacts your search engine rankings and visibility. Off-page optimization is everything that you do off of your website that directly influences and impacts your search engine rankings and visibility. I extensively go over the factors that are involved in on-page and off-page optimization in my book entitled: **Search Engine Domination: The Ultimate Secrets to Increasing Your Website's Visibility and Making a Ton of Cash.**

Traffic

Traffic is the lifeblood of any online business. It doesn't matter if you have a great product or service if your website does not have any traffic there is no way that you can make any money from it. You generate traffic to your website through the efforts of your marketing online as well as offline. However, you just don't want to generate any kind of traffic, you want to generate targeted traffic.

Targeted traffic consists of people who are in your niche market and who are interested in the type of products and services that you have to offer. These people are more likely to buy from you and become your customers. The bottom line is you need a consistent and continuous flow of targeted traffic to your website in order to have a sustainable and thriving online business. The following are online and offline methods that you can use to generate traffic to your website.

Online Methods of Generating Traffic

Banner Advertising

Banner advertising can be an effective way of driving traffic to your site and increasing your brand's awareness. A banner ad is basically a form of advertising that involves the embedding of an advertisement in a web page. The actual banner which contains your advertisement comes in all kinds of different shapes and sizes. The more popular shapes are the rectangular, square and button shaped banners. The more popular sizes include the 468 X 60, 728 X 90, 250 X 250, 125 X 125, 120 X 90 and the 120 X 60.

Banner ads can also contain audio, video and animation and the way that it is utilized in advertising is the banner ad is strategically placed alongside the content of the site that you wish to advertise on. The way that you receive traffic to your website via the banner ad is a HTML code containing the URL address of your website is inserted into the banner. When someone clicks on that banner they get automatically directed to your website.

In order for your banner ad to be effective it must be visually appealing, have an attractive message and be targeted to the right audience. The best way to purchase banner advertising is through a banner ad network such as Adbrite located at http://www.adbrite.com or Chitika located at http:// www.Chitika.com.

Ezine Advertising

First of all let me explain what an Ezine is. An Ezine is an electronic newsletter or magazine that is delivered via email or made available online. There are all kinds of Ezines out there that cater to various niches which make them ideal, because you are able to find the right targeted audience for your particular products and services. For example, if you were in the health and fitness business, there are Ezines that cater to that specific type of audience. Same thing if you were in the business of selling dog products and related accessories, there are Ezines out there that cater to that market and have subscribers that would be interested in what you have to offer.

The easy way to locate the Ezines that are in your online business's niche is through

Charlie Page's Directory of Ezines located at www.directoryofEzines.com. There are mainly 3 different Ezine advertising options that are available so let's review them.

- **Classifieds** – Classified ads are usually 3 to 6 lines in length and are relatively inexpensive. Personally, I have had success driving traffic to my various websites using classified Ezine advertising, but compared to the other advertising options available I find it to be the least effective primarily because they are grouped with so many other classified ads that are also vying for the same attention.

- **Sponsor ads** – Sponsor ads are considered to be prime real estate in the Ezine advertising world because they are located at the very top of the Ezine issue which gives it more eyeballs and visibility. Sponsor ads cost more than classified ads, but they are worth it because they are usually more effective.

- **Solo ads** – Solo ads are stand alone ads that an Ezine sends out separately from their issues to their subscribers. Solo ads are basically short sales letters that allow you to explain in detail what you are offering. Solo ads offer you the most exposure so obviously they are going

to cost more than the classified or
sponsor ads.

Article Marketing

The writing of articles and submitting
them to the many thousands of article
directories online is another effective way
that you can drive a humongous amount of
traffic to your website and also establish
yourself as an expert or authority in your
particular niche. Article marketing also helps
to increase your website's search engine
ranking because it produces backlinks (other
sites linking to you) which is a determining
factor in search engine rankings.

The way that you get backlinks and
traffic to your website is at the end of every
article there is a resource box where you can
enter information about your business and
include a link back to your website. Usually
after people have finished reading your
article and have found it to be informative
they will click on the link located in the
resource box that leads to your website to
find out more.

Online Press Releases

Online press releases are a great way to
get publicity for your business. They are also
a great way to generate traffic to your
website and also a great way to increase your
search engine rankings which leads to more
traffic to your website. There are many free

as well as paid press release submissions sites that will distribute your press releases. However, the advantage of using a paid submission service is that the major ones such as PRWeb will send your press release to the major media outlets that the company has a direct relationship with. This will enable your press release to get full exposure and high visibility if it is quality written and newsworthy.

Press releases can also be a great way to attract interested radio show producers and many other people looking for interviews which can result in the opportunity for you to share your expertise with their audience. When this opportunity presents itself, seize the moment by plugging your business and your website which will drive traffic to it. Just like an article, an online press release can contain a link that leads back to your website.

Social Media

I'm quite sure that you are already familiar with social media sites like Facebook, Twitter, Google+ and LinkedIn and how they let you connect with your family, friends and in the case of LinkedIn your network of business contacts, but keep in mind that these social media sites can also be a good source for getting traffic to your website. However, you don't want to spam people or be conspicuous with your intentions. Instead you want to take a more subtle approach like posting or tweeting information that will help others. Once you have built that kind of reputation and credibility, you can then start to gradually post information about your business and links that lead back to your website.

In the case of Facebook, you can also use Facebook Ads to drive traffic to your website. LinkedIn also offers advertising options to drive traffic to your site.

YouTube

YouTube receives over 800 million unique viewers per month and it is an excellent place to utilize to draw traffic to your website by creating and uploading informative and entertaining videos. If applicable you can make tutorial and "How to" videos or you can create videos about the products and services that you have to offer on your website. The way that you get traffic to your website is by mentioning your website in your videos or by putting your website's address in the description area of the video.

You can also create a YouTube channel for your business and this will allow you to send out emails to your subscribers where you can mention your website to generate traffic.

Pay Per Click Advertising

If you really want to drive targeted traffic to your website quickly, then pay per click advertising is your best option. In fact, it takes less than 10 minutes to receive traffic from around the world once you've signed up. Pay per click advertising is a method for generating traffic wherein you pay for every visitor that goes to your website as a result of clicking on your ad, hence the name pay per click.

The most notable pay per click advertising program is Google Adwords. Another popular pay per click program is the Microsoft Advertising Ad Center platform which incorporates both Bing and Yahoo search engines. The cost that you pay per click with this type of advertising is determined by the competitive bid that you placed on particular keywords that are relevant to your website. For example, say that you have a website that sells golf clubs and you placed a bid of .70 cents for that particular keyword. It will cost you .70 cents or less whenever someone clicks on your ad that showed up as a result of them typing in the keyword "golf clubs".

The reason why I say it might cost you less than .70 cents is because there are other factors that come into play such as what others have bid for the same keyword. Let's say that the average bid was .55 cents. Even though you bid .70 cents you will be only charged .55 cents. Other factors such as your quality score and your click thru rate will also determine whether you are going to pay less than the .70 cents that you originally bid when advertising on Google Adwords.

Another great benefit of pay per click advertising is that you only spend what your budget allows. You can scale up or down as you please.

Offline Methods of Generating Traffic

There are many offline marketing tactics that you can utilize to drive traffic to your website. You can advertise in the newspapers, magazines, radio and even television to drive traffic to your website. Other offline marketing methods to drive traffic to your website include participating and organizing community events, holding workshops and seminars that are designed to build a rapport with your target audience and familiarize them with the products and services that you offer on your website.

In addition to these methods, you can also purchase a mailing list from a mailing list broker that consists of people who have already shown an interest or have purchased similar products and services as yours. Once you have obtained your mailing list you can use direct mail to solicit your prospects and drive them to your website. Direct mail contains a marketing message in a printed format such as a letter, postcard, self mailer, flyer and brochure and is sent via mail to elicit a response from the people that have received them.

A direct mail campaign is usually designed to send its recipients to what is called a squeeze page which is a one page website that has the sole purpose of capturing their information for follow-up marketing. In fact, a squeeze page is definitely an online business essential.

Chapter 8- Online Business Models

There are several business models in which to choose from when starting an online business and the great thing is you are not confined to or limited to one choice or one business. In fact, you can utilize and employ several different business models simultaneously and produce multiple streams of income. The path that you take of course is entirely up to you. In this chapter, I will discuss in detail the online business models, the advantages that each have to offer and how to generate revenue from them.

The Affiliate Model

The affiliate model in my opinion is the easiest online business model, because it doesn't require any significant amount of capital to get started with. As an affiliate you will promote products and services for companies and when your promotion results in a sale you earn a commission for your efforts. As an affiliate marketer you can also get paid per click for every time that you send traffic to a merchant's website or you can make money when someone takes a specific action on a merchant's website as a result of your promotion like filling out a form, signing up for a special event etc.

There are numerous advantages in starting your own affiliate marketing business and here are a few them:

You can work from anywhere. All you need is an internet connection and you can basically run your affiliate business from anywhere.

There are little or no risks involved. The risks are minimal in operating an affiliate business. Of course with any business you have to monitor your expenses to minimize your exposure to risk and the only significant expense that you will have is spending money to acquire traffic to your website which constitutes your marketing costs. The great thing about investing money in generating traffic is that you can always scale it down if needed, or you can switch your concentration to generating traffic organically through the search engines, which is somewhat free. You can even generate traffic through social media.

The great thing about having an affiliate business is that you are not bound to any type of long term contract. This is beneficial to you because if something is not selling or doesn't work, you can simply stop selling and promoting it. No harm, no foul.

Your affiliate business runs on autopilot. The great thing about being an affiliate marketer is once you have your affiliate system set up along with your marketing and promotions, you make money automatically even while you're asleep because your website is operating 24/7.

No technical or sales experience is necessary. Most merchants supply you with the marketing materials that you need so you don't have to create them yourself. These marketing materials are in the form of banners, pre-written email messages, articles etc., plus other materials that are designed to educate your prospects about the products or services that are being offered by the merchants with the intention of getting a sale or getting the prospect to perform some specific action that will result in you making a commission.

You don't have to have your own product. Creating your own product from scratch, can be burdensome and costly, by becoming an affiliate marketer you leave the product creation to others while you share in the revenues. How wonderful is that?

No customer headaches. All customer orders and inquiries are dealt with by the merchant. You don't have to deal with the customer or be bothered with customer service.

There is no inventory involved. You won't have a ton of boxes of inventory sitting in your house or garage hoping to get rid of them because this is an inventory free business.

There are minimal costs involved: The costs that are associated with operating an affiliate business are the costs of building a website or a blog (that should be no more than $200 - $300), the cost of purchasing the domain name for your website or blog (no more than $12 /year), hosting (no more than $7 a month), an autoresponder message system so that you can capture and follow up with your leads (no more than $19 per month), content creation for your site which can be outsourced at the price of $5 an article and as mentioned previously the costs associated with marketing which varies.

To get started in creating your affiliate business here are the steps that you must take.

Step 1. Market Research – You have to perform market research and your research should involve finding out what products that people want or are searching for. You can get this information by using the Google Keyword Planner or some other tool or software that will allow you to put in keyword search terms and enable you to generate those answers. You don't want to waste your time, money and energy trying to market products as an affiliate that are not commercially viable or there is only lukewarm demand.

In addition, you should also spend time researching the various affiliate programs that exists. Inspect what they have to offer you—their terms, products, commission rates, etc.

Step 2. Join Your Affiliate Programs – Once you have done your research and due diligence on the various affiliate programs, your next step would be to join the ones that interest you. Once you have joined, you would get your affiliate ID and the associated marketing materials to promote the merchants and products that you chose.

Step 3. Create a Content Based Website - Now that you know the type of products you will be promoting, it is time for you to create a content based website that will attract the targeted visitors that you need to make affiliate sales. Your content should be relevant to the products that you are promoting. For example, if you are promoting weight loss products you should have content on your site that specifically discusses how to lose weight.

Very few people reach a web site with the intention of clicking on an affiliate button and spending money. It is well written content that attracts visitors and then converts these visitors into buyers which will result in affiliate income for you. So it is important that you create content that has value and provides relevant information that your visitors or your website's subscribers will benefit from. Once they feel that have benefitted from your content this will strongly influence them to click on your affiliate links which should be well position around your content.

Step 4. Put your affiliate links, banners etc., on your website, blog, articles, newsletters and emails.

Once you have your content based website completed, you can now populate it with your affiliate links, banners and marketing materials. You must also remember to include your affiliate links in your email correspondence, as well as in the newsletters, e-books or articles that you are using to promote your affiliate products.

Step 5. Marketing your website - Once you have your website up and running with your affiliate links it is time for you to market your website and drive traffic to it. Please refer to the last chapter in the section where I covered the various ways in which you can utilize to drive traffic to your website.

Step 6. Make money - When you have effectively implemented steps 1-5, the reward for your effort is making money. Now the amount that you make depends entirely on the demand of the products that you are promoting, their price point, and the percentage of commission that you will earn as a result of a successful action taking place.

There are many people today who are making a boatload of cash from the affiliate business model and if you're serious about it and are willing to put in the required effort you can too. You don't necessarily have to create a stand alone affiliate business meaning that it is your only online business and therefore your only revenue source. You can also use the affiliate model as a supplemental income source to augment your main online business.

Now the smart way to do this is to choose to promote affiliate products that are complementary to what you are offering on your website. For example, if you are selling fitness DVDs, you might also want to be an affiliate of products such as supplements or vitamins or other related products because they are complementary and in line with what you are already offering.

To get you up and running quickly, here are a few affiliate networks that you can join and look for products to promote:

- **Amazon Associates** - Amazon associates (aka affiliates) drive traffic to Amazon.com via specially formatted links that allow Amazon to track sales. Associates are paid up to 10% referral fees on qualifying revenue that is generated by their affiliate links.

- **Commission Junction** – Commission Junction offers a slew of different companies and products that you can promote as an affiliate. As with practically all affiliate networks, Commission Junction is free to join and once you have signed up you can then opt into the different affiliate programs that are available.

- **Clickbank** – If you would like to promote digital products then Clickbank is your affiliate solution. It is basically the number one destination for affiliates who are seeking to promote digital products and make money. There are over 10,000 merchants in which you can choose to promote products from.

The Information Products Model

You can create an online business that is based on the dissemination and selling of information. In the simplest terms, an information product is a product that provides a solution to an existing problem. For example, it can be an ebook that shows people how to get out of financial debt or an instructional DVD or CD that teaches people how to speak Spanish. In addition to these formats an information product can also be packaged as a PDF, an MP3 audio, a webinar or teleseminar or as a home study course.

If you are an expert at something you can build an entire business around your expertise. You can create various information products for your particular niche audience and sell them directly from your website and you can also sell them through other popular platforms such as Ebay, Amazon and Clickbank. As your customers devour your information products and they are completely satisfied with the content that you have provided, you immediately become an authority figure perception wise in their eyes. This will enable you to create a consulting service based on your expertise and offer it to them ,which represents another income stream for you.

But what if you are not an expert on anything? Can you still create an information business? The answer is yes and there many creative ways that you can accomplish this. You can of course outsource the task and let other people create the information product for you. You can also interview actual experts from various niches and create information products based on those interviews.

For example, you could interview and record several Ebay Powersellers and create information products in different formats and sell them. You can create an ebook, audio CDs, MP3 audio, a home study course and even a DVD video if you managed to film the interviews. You can call this particular information product something like **"Conversations with Ebay Powersellers: Secrets Revealed"** and you would make a mint.

Don't worry about stealing this particular idea because I have plenty more that I won't be revealing. I'm just sharing this one with you to get your creative juices flowing and to expose you to a whole new level of thinking and possibilities when you choose to create an online business based on the information products business model.

So let's go through the process of how you would actually go about creating this **"Conversations with Ebay Powersellers: Secrets Revealed"** information product. First, you would have to find some Ebay Powersellers to interview. The way to find Ebay Powersellers to interview is by simply looking for them on Ebay. They are not hard to find because they are easily identified by the Powerseller logo next to their Ebay user name. All you would have to do is contact them through the Ebay message system and ask them can you interview them.

When you get a few of them to agree to the interview have them sign an agreement that states that they have given you consent to record the interview and you have the right to use the product anyway you see fit. You can compensate them financially if you like, but truthfully it's not necessary to take that approach. Most of these Powersellers would jump at the chance of being interviewed and showcased as an expert. Plus, you can convey the benefits of participating in your interview such as an opportunity to promote their Ebay store and the products that they sell to a wider audience etc.

Make sure that you stipulate in your agreement the financial terms if you decide to go that route. If you pay them a flat fee for participating in the interview make sure that your agreement indicates that after the flat fee is paid they won't receive any further payment from you. If you decide to take my suggestion of not compensating them financially you must disclose that the product that will be created from these interviews will be commercially available for sale and they won't receive any royalty payments just exposure as compensation. I would suggest that you consult with a lawyer on this matter. If some of the Powersellers disagree to this, move on and find those who will agree to this arrangement.

Now that you have taken care of the legal stuff, it is now time to prepare for the interviews. Preparation is key if you want to get a great interview from each Ebay Powerseller. Preparation involves setting goals. You should be clear on what you want to achieve from the interviews and once you have established this you want to communicate your goals to your interviewees beforehand.

Preparation also involves doing some research on the topic so that you have a basic understanding of the subject matter. Once you have done your homework and familiarized yourself with the topic, you can now create a list of questions to ask. When creating your list of questions make sure that they are open-ended. For example, you would ask "What difficulties do Ebay Powersellers have to overcome?" Instead of "Is it difficult to become an Ebay Powerseller?" The latter is a closed ended question that can be answered with a simple "yes" or "no".

You should create an adequate amount of questions so that you have more than enough content for the information product that you are going to create from your series of interviews. Once you have done that you have to decide on the necessary hardware or software that you will be using to record the interview. You can use the video recording features of Skype if you want to create a product that has visuals. The beauty of Skype is that it allows you to record a video without having to be on the premises to film the interview. All it takes is for you and your interviewees to have a web camera, a microphone, and the sharing tools that Skype provides and you are ready to go. Skype is free and easy to use.

You can also record your interviews via telephone, but you will need a telephone recorder. You can purchase a telephone recorder at a company called Dynametric located at http://www.dynametric.com. Dynametric also has telephone software that will even allow you to record your cell phone conversations. It is recommended that you use a recorder of high quality and you must make sure it has ease of use and the capabilities to convert your audio to a suitable format like Wav, AIIF, or an MP3 format. This will allow you to make audio CDs and other related audio products.

When you have everything that you need, it's time to arrange and conduct the interviews. Once the interviews have been recorded and edited, it's time to create your information products. If you are creating an ebook from the recordings all you have to do is use a transcription service. The transcription service will transcribe word for word the audio for you and put it in text format such as in a Word Document. Once you have it in a Word Document you can then use Adobe Acrobat Pro or some other software to convert it to a PDF file. Once you have converted it to a PDF file you now have an ebook.

You can offer your ebook on your website for sale as a downloadable PDF file and you can also sell it on Clickbank as well as other venues. You can take those same audio recordings and make CDs from them or you can offer it as MP3 audio download on your website if you prefer not to be bothered with the process of shipping CDs. The other types of information products that you can create from your interviews are DVDs and a home study course.

A home study course consists of content that allows its' users to study the materials conveniently from the comforts of their own home or place of choice. A home study course is a bigger package than an ebook so you can charge a much higher price for it because of the perceived value. A home study course mainly consists of a manual in a three ring loose leaf binder that is accompanied by CDs or DVDs or a combination of the three.

Let me give you an example of how lucrative selling your information product as a home study course can be for you. Sticking with the same example let's say that you turned your **"Conversations with Ebay Powersellers: Secrets Revealed"** interviews into a home study course. First of all, there are very little upfront costs associated with creating a home study course because you will be using the "print on demand" model. "Print on demand" simply means you will only print or manufacture the home study course when you have received orders for it. You will carry no inventory and the money that you collect from the sales will be used to purchase what you need to manufacture and ship the course.

You can manufacture your home study course directly from your home all you need is a capable computer and printer that will also allow you to print CDs or DVDs from it. Epson offers a line of printers that have that capability. Of course you will also need blank printable CDs or DVDs, 3-hole copy paper and a 3 ring binder to produce your final product. Here are the typical costs associated with producing a home study course that consists of 6 audio CDs and a manual.

There's a place that I use call NRS Recording Supplies that sells 100 ink jet printable CDs for only $20 and with the shipping the total cost of the CDs are $29 which works out to .29 cents per CD. You only will be using 6 CDs in our example so your total cost per CD is $1.74 (6 X .29 cents =$1.74). The 3 ring loose leaf binder from your local office supply store will cost about $4. The price for a ream of 500 sheet 3-hole copy paper will cost around $8. Let's say that your manual contains 200 sheets of paper. Your cost per page rounded off to the nearest cent will approximately be .02 cents. So for 200 pages it will cost you $4.

So let's add our numbers up and for simplicity purposes we won't get too detailed and include the cost of the amount of ink that you will expend when you print one copy. $1.74 + $4 + $4 = $9.74. You decide to sell your home study course for $297 your profit excluding your marketing costs will be a whopping $287.26 per unit sold. How amazing is that?

In concluding the information products business model the benefits are numerous and quite obvious as to why you would consider adopting this particular model to build your online business.

Selling Digital Products Model

I have already covered some of this topic in our discussion of the information products business model when I highlighted ebooks, and MP3 audio. These represent digital products. In short, digital products are anything that can be delivered online whether it is music, software, images, videos etc. There are many advantages that exist for you if you adopt this particular model for your online business. Here are a few of those advantages:

1) **No running out of stock** – With digital products you'll never run out of stock because once you have created your digital product and have uploaded it to your website or any other venue it can be downloaded over and over again which leads me to the second advantage.

2) **There's no shipping involved** – Your digital product is automatically delivered online so you don't have worry about shipping costs or standing on line at the Post Office which leads me to the third advantage.

3) **Runs on autopilot** – Once you have uploaded your digital product and your customers have paid for it they can automatically and securely access it from your website or any other venue that you sell from without any human intervention 24/7.

4) **Creates Passive income** – Selling digital products allow you to create passive income. Passive income is money that you earn consistently for a long period of time for effort you put in once.

5) **Scalability** – Once you have your infrastructure set up, it is easy to scale your digital product. You can easily position yourself to sell 10,000 units or 1 million units and no additional work is required in regards to product creation.

There's a lot of money to be made selling digital products, how much money you make as with anything is determined by how big your vision is and whether you execute. A perfect example of someone having a big vision and the ability to execute is Shutterstock's founder Jon Oringer who became a billionaire simply by licensing images online. He built an online business from scratch and got it to the point where he was able to take his company public and make a mint.

Does the whole idea of creating an online business based on the digital products business model appeal to you now? Are you starting to envision the numerous opportunities that exist in this field? If so and you are short on ideas here are a few that you should consider building a business around.

Clip Art

WordPress Plugins

Music

Tutorials

Recipes

Online Newsletters

Open Source Scripts

Desktop Apps

Smart Phone Apps

Web Graphics

Podcasts

Now that you have some ideas to get you started you will need a secure way of delivering your digital products to your customers without a hassle. For that task you should strongly consider using a digital selling service. A digital selling service takes care of the storage of your digital product, the payment as well as the delivery of it. Here is an example of how it actually works:

1) You upload your digital product to the digital service's secure server.

2) Your customer clicks on the buy now button on your website which is

integrated with the digital service provider that you have chosen.

3) Your customer pays for your product.

4) They are then redirected to a secure download page provided by the digital service provider where they are then able to download your digital product.

Let's go back to step 3 when your customer pays for your product. When your customer pays for the product, the digital service provider does not go through the big credit card companies directly to process the payment. Instead they go through payment processors such as Paypal, Google Checkout, 2Checkout, Amazon Payments as well as others.

This allows your customers to pay using a variety of methods such as credit cards, eChecks, and ACH transfers. The digital service provider immediately remits the money from the sale to you. However, they charge a fee for doing so. These fees vary among digital service providers and you have to do your own due diligence in this regard. Here are a few digital service providers in which you can choose from.

Sellfy

Payloadz

E-Junkie

FetchApp

Goodsie

PulleyApp

DPD

Plimus

Selling Physical Products Model

You can choose the online business model of selling physical products from your website or through other venues. You can create these products yourself or you can sell products that are manufactured by other companies. Personally, I have done both. I've already discussed my experience with using the dropshipping method to sell products manufactured by others.

Some of the cons of using dropshipping are you don't have 100% control in terms of the pricing and manufacturing of the product. There were numerous times where I have sold products using the dropshipping method only to find out that the dropshipping company ran out of stock resulting in me having to refund my customers. Now I'm not saying that this will be the case with all dropshipping companies, but what I am saying is you're not in total control. Keep this in mind if you're contemplating using the dropshipping method to sell physical products.

Another alternative to dropshipping is buying private label products and reselling them from your website or through other online channels. What is the concept behind a private label product? Private label companies make products, and then in turn sell these products to other entities (like your online business), who then sell them under their own brand name. The great benefit of utilizing private labels are that it allows you to market pre-manufactured, pre-tested products as your own.

Private label products afford you more control than dropshipping, because you have the product in your possession and you can increase or decrease your inventory as you see fit. There is also freedom in pricing your products and if you want you can modify them as you wish.

The major difference between selling physical products versus selling digital products is that physical products are much more harder to scale and there also can be geographical limitations when it comes to shipping. For example, let's say that you have a product selling for $25 and it weighs 8 pounds. When you ship that product within the United States your costs are reasonable, but it's an entirely different story cost wise if you want to ship that same exact product outside of the country. As with any of the online business models mentioned here you should weigh the pros and cons of selling physical products before proceeding forward.

Membership Model

If you like receiving recurring revenue then the membership model can be ideal for you. The membership model is subscription based where your members pay you on a continuous basis to have access to information on your website. This could be videos, audio, relevant content or pretty much anything that they are willing to pay for on a continuous basis.

The membership model could include having access to services such as coaching or software. It can also be in the form of a community where you have a membership based forum where people can log in and chat with other people with similar interests or it could even be a support forum where you give your members help on an ongoing basis. As you can clearly see there are a slew of options available when choosing this particular model.

The key to being successful with the membership model is being able to consistently provide valuable information, content or services to your members. Another key is you want to be able to understand the main reasons why people want to be members and stay on as members because it is only natural that they will be asking themselves those same exact questions, especially when they are charged that recurring payment every month or whenever you charge them. Even if you offer quality content or excellent service you are still going to get some people who will cancel their membership.

Here are a few things that you should consider when implementing the membership model for your online business.

1) **Determining the best membership site for you** – As I previously mentioned there are a slew of options and different types of membership models that you can choose from. You can deliver consultant services through your membership site, software, content etc. Some of the questions you should be asking yourself are: Do you want to offer just content? Do you want to offer just services? Or do you want to offer a combination of both?

2) **Your goals** - Once you have decided on the type of membership site that you will be offering you have to figure out your goals as to what you want to accomplish with your site as well as the topic. Of course the obvious goals are to make money and to build a strong rapport with your members, but I'm sure there are other important goals that you would like to accomplish with your site.

3) **Creation and delivery of content** – Obviously you need content for your membership site and you have to decide whether you will be creating the content yourself or outsourcing that task. You

have to also decide what format you will be delivering your content in. Will it be video? Audio? Plain text? By the telephone?(if you're consulting) or will it involve multiple formats?

Other things that you have to consider are how often will you be delivering your content to your members? Will it be weekly, monthly, bi-monthly, quarterly or yearly? Whatever you decide, you have to make sure that you consistently deliver high quality content.

4) **Membership price** – You have to decide on a price for the membership that you are offering. You have to price your membership at an amount that makes sense for both you and your members. Remember that you will be providing valuable content to your members and you shouldn't hesitate when determining a price for that value. Price your membership to low and people will think strangely enough that it can't possibly be of any value to them. Price it too high relative to the content that you are offering and people simply won't sign up to become members.

To entice people to sign up as members you should offer a free trial membership, a sort of "try it before you buy it" irresistible type of offer. Once they've tried it and they like it their free membership will automatically convert to a paid membership once their free trial is over.

5) **Creating your membership site** – Your membership site can be easily created by using software for that particular task. If you go that route rather than choosing a website designer to build it for you there are many membership site software options available in which to choose from. Here are a few of those options.

Wordpress (and a membership plugin like Wishlist)

Joomla

aMember

Services Model

Do you have an expertise that is commercially viable and can benefit others? If your answer is yes, then the services online business model will suit you well. In fact, you don't even have to be an expert at anything to reap the benefits of this business model, you can outsource whatever you don't know.

For example, if you want to create a business designing websites and you personally don't have the skills to do so, you can outsource that task to a reliable freelancer who does. The key with this approach is you have to be able to negotiate favorable prices with your freelancer to ensure that you make a nice profit. You have to be able to "buy low" and "sell high" so to speak.

The services business model compliments the information products model very well and you can utilize them both at the same time. For instance, after your customers have bought something informative from you like a "How to" ebook you can upsell them to a coaching program. Most savvy online marketers usually create ebooks with the purpose of attracting people to their coaching programs.

In addition to coaching, here are some other services that you can offer online:

Video Editing

Audio Editing

Virtual Assistance

Resume Writing

Business Plan Writing

Graphic Arts

Logo Creation

Voiceovers

Copywriting

Programming

Technical Work

SEO Services

Language Translation

Transcriptions

Bookkeeping

Marketing

Advertising Model

This particular online business model can be utilized in two different ways. It can either be your main business and primary source of revenue or it can be used to generate secondary income to support your main business. The advertising online business model is quite similar to the television, print media and radio advertising model in the offline world in that the amount of money that you charge people to advertise on your platform be it on your website or some sort of online newsletter will be based on the total amount of subscribers that you have or how much traffic you are receiving at your website.

The advertising online business model is usually based around a website that has content and provides valuable information to others. This is how you attract the necessary traffic to your site which is a perquisite to sell advertising. Your website should focus on a specific niche so that you are not all over the place and you can gain traction and visibility in the search engines by using laser focused targeted keywords. The niche that you choose should be a fairly popular one or you risk the possibility of not generating enough traffic which will be the death of your advertising business.

There are many ways that you can charge for advertising on your website and here are a few of those ways:

Cost per thousand impressions (CPM) – This is a traditional way to charge for ads online. The advertiser is charged per thousand impressions. The way that impressions work is each time a unique user visits a page that has the client ad an impression is recorded. For example, let's say that an advertiser's ad placed on the home page of your website receives 20,000 unique visits and your ad rate was $9 cost per thousand, you will bill that client $180 (20 X 9) for advertising on your website.

Cost per action (CPA) – The way that cost per action works is the advertiser is charged every time a visitor makes a transaction or purchases a product. As the website owner you can either set the price for the action or you can let your advertiser choose their price.

Cost per click (CPC) - The advertiser is charged every time someone clicks on their ads. It's that simple. You basically set the price as to what they will be charged per click.

Flat rate – With the flat rate model the advertiser is charged a fixed amount for placing an ad on your website. If your traffic isn't steady or isn't big enough for the cost per thousands impressions model to work for you profit wise then you should start off with the flat rate model.

A great way to generate money using the advertising model for your business is by creating an Ezine and selling advertising. As I mentioned previously, an Ezine is an electronic newsletter or magazine that is delivered via email or made available online. The amount of money you can charge for advertising in your Ezine is usually based on the amount of subscribers that you have. The quickest way to build your subscriber base is by offering a free subscription to your Ezine as a reward for signing up. You can also accelerate the amount of subscribers that you have by joining several Ezine co-ops.

The primary purpose for an Ezine co-op is to send subscribers your way. Ezine co-ops have several types of business models, so you should investigate the one that will work best for you. One method that they use to generate subscribers for you is by allowing people to place a free ad in your Ezine as an enticement to become a subscriber to your Ezine.

Once they have signed up through the co-op to place a free ad, the co-op then sends you those subscribers' names and email addresses along with their free classified ads. You would then contact those subscribers and inform them that they have been added to your subscribers list and give them the date when their free classified ad will run.

I've already discussed the different ways to advertise in Ezines if you wanted to generate traffic to your website and those same exact ways you would use to also sell advertising in your particular Ezine. Once again here are those different forms of advertising that you can offer.

Classified ads

Sponsor ads

Solo ads

You don't necessarily have to create your own Ezine to build a subscriber's list and sell advertising online. As mentioned earlier you can also build a list of subscribers by offering various free reports via multiple squeeze pages as an enticement to get people to subscribe to your email list. Once you have gained a fair amount of subscribers you can then charge advertisers money to send out their particular sales messages to your list so that they will be able to not only advertise their products and services, but to also build their own list of subscribers.

The way that this process works is they will have some sort of free report, presentation or software to offer as a way to entice people to join their list. They would then craft their sales message and give that message to you in a text file that highlights what they are specifically giving away for free and a link leading to their squeeze page. You would then take that sales message and send it out to your list of subscribers of course for a fee. You will guarantee that they will receive a certain amount of unique clicks to their sign up page that contains their free offer. This of course will be tracked and you will issue them a report after you have run their ad campaign.

I must note that you are guaranteeing the amount of unique clicks that they will receive and not the conversions, but if you have a pretty responsive list of subscribers, conversions shouldn't be a problem because there is a free offer involved so people will be eager to sign up. The process that I've just described is called Solo ad advertising and it can be very lucrative, but it requires you to be able to build a nice size list of subscribers. As the saying goes "the money is in the list".

To give you an idea of what you can charge others to send out solo ads to your list of subscribers here are some typical solo ad rates that I have paid to solo ad providers in the past to send out my free offers to their list.

200 Click Solo Ad $80

500 Click Solo Ad $175

1,000 Click Solo Ad $400

2,000 Click Solo Ad $650

3,000 Click Solo Ad $950

If you are interested in finding solo ad providers that will enable you build a huge list of subscribers fast I have the Internet Marketer's Solo Ad Directory available at

http://www.makeprofitseasy.com/soloads.html

In concluding this topic, needless to say you have a myriad of choices available when choosing a model or multiple models for your online business. I have covered in detail the main ones, but make sure that you investigate further and perform your own due diligence before making your final choice. Also if you want to test the waters before investing a chunk of capital into an online business I suggest reading my book entitled **How to Start an Online Business with Less Than $200.**

Chapter 9: Funding Your Online Startup

There are several options to consider when looking to fund your online business startup. Some of the options may be obvious to you and some may not. Some may apply to your situation or some may not depending on how small or large your business will be. An entrepreneur's ability to raise capital efficiently will strongly determine whether their business succeeds or fail so it is important that we review the funding options.

Savings – This is the obvious place where you should look to fund your business startup. If you can't invest some of the money that you have in your savings into your business then you lack confidence, therefore you should consider sticking with your day job. If you're not willing to invest in yourself and your ideas don't expect others to. Plus interest rates are at an all time low and if you have money just sitting in the bank earning little or no interest inflation will eat it up. So, why not invest that money into your business instead and earn a return on your investment?

There are many advantages to using the money that you have in your savings to fund your startup.

1) **You don't have to ask anyone else for the money** – You can bootstrap your way to success as many entrepreneurs before you

have done. It takes dedication, discipline, and personal sacrifice, but if you are up for the challenge then go for it!

2) **You are not starting out in debt** – Having no debt represents freedom. You don't have to worry about paying someone a weekly or monthly payment for loaning you the money which hinders the cash flow aspects of your business. By tapping your savings you also avoid paying interest charges and giving equity in your business away at an early stage.

3) **It shows to others that you are committed** – Later on you may want to pump more cash into your business to grow it and this requires an investment from others. It's appealing to these investors if you have some of your own skin invested in the game. It shows them that you are committed to your business venture enough because you put your own financial weight behind it.

Friends and Family – Friends and family can be a great source of financial support for your business. They are more likely to give you generous terms than people who you barely know. However, you have to be careful that you honor your commitment to them and vice versa or this may lead to irreparable damage to the relationship.

Angel Investors – Angel investors are people who provide capital for a business startup usually in exchange for a piece of the equity. If you decide to take this route to raise capital please be aware that some angel investors may want to take on an active role in your business. If you have a problem with that you should choose angel investors who don't mind being silent partners.

Venture Capital – If you're really thinking big you should consider venture capital as a funding source. However, it is extremely difficult to get venture capital when you are pre-revenue or in the early stages of your business. You should seek venture capital when you have proven your business model with sales and you have a viable exit strategy.

Venture capitalist deal in millions so if you are only seeking a small amount of capital this is not the best option for you. Venture capitalist make high risk, high return investments and are looking to find those startups that have the most potential for an initial public offering (IPO) or have a chance of being acquired by a bigger company.

Credit Cards – Many successful entrepreneurs have funded their business using credit cards. Although this is not the ideal way to fund a business because of the obvious drawbacks like high interest rates and the possibility of becoming too overleveraged it can be a useful option if you use it wisely. As soon as it becomes economically feasible for you, you should immediately pay off any outstanding credit card balances because it is the prudent thing to do.

Funding and growing a business through sales – This is the most risk adverse way to start and run a business. The way that it would work is you get paid in advance before you buy the product to deliver it to your customers or you get paid before you render a service. I must admit that this is a slow way to grow your business, but sometimes it can be the wisest.

Crowd Funding – Crowd funding is the collective effort of individuals who network and pool their money, usually via the Internet, to support efforts initiated by other people or organizations. Crowd funding in my opinion is one of the most creative ways to fund a business and the great thing is you don't have to pay the money back and you don't have to give up any equity! One of the most popular places to raise money through crowd funding via the internet is on a site called Kickstarter.com.

The way that Kickstarter works is this. You would list your project describing in detail what is and then you would state the amount of funding you are seeking. If people like your project and are interested, they pledge money to make it happen. The funding is all or nothing meaning that the project must meet its funding goal in its entirety for you to receive the money that was pledged.

What do the people who pledge the money receive? They receive some type of reward from the project creator. For example, backers of an effort to make a book or film often get a copy of the finished work.

There are many creative ways to fund a business and I hope that I have provided you with enough helpful options in which to choose from.

Chapter 10: Don't Quit Your Day Job Just Yet

For some people it makes perfect sense for them to keep their day job while working on their entrepreneurial endeavors while other people might find that working at a job is a complete hindrance in pursuing and realizing their entrepreneurial vision. I don't know what the particular case maybe for you, but whatever decision that you make in terms of whether to quit your job or not should be well thought out especially if other people like a significant other or your family will be impacted by your decision.

For example, if you have a family it would be extremely tough for you to just up and quit your job to start an online business unless you have a substantial amount of savings to tide you over until you are able to generate enough income from your online business to cover your basic living expenses.

I know that many people tend to get caught up in the hype of stories of those entrepreneurs who came up with a great idea for a product, service or business and immediately quit their day job to successfully bring into fruition their entrepreneurial vision. Although some entrepreneurs have taken this path and achieved success, the vast majority of entrepreneurs work at their day jobs until the revenue that they're making from their entrepreneurial venture comes close to or exceeds the income that they're making from their job. Case in point, Steve Jobs and Steve Wozniak worked for the video company Atari while founding Apple.

The bottom line is, whether you decide to quit your job or not (and I'm not telling you to do so) is entirely up to you and should be based on what your gut instinct is telling you and what your personal circumstances are in terms of family, finances, and where you are at in your life.

For instance, maybe you are working at a menial or dead end job that is going nowhere and you actually feel that you would gain a great deal more and benefit by quitting your lousy job right on the spot to start your online business. Maybe you are just plain tired of all the years of you hemming and hawing waiting for the perfect moment to quit and you believe it's in your best interest to act now or never.

Conversely, sometimes a once in a lifetime opportunity presents itself and the only way for you to take full advantage of it and capitalize on it is by quitting your job immediately and focusing on that opportunity regardless of your circumstances. However, this requires courage and the ability to reach deep down inside of yourself to come up with creative solutions, financial or otherwise that will allow you to pursue that opportunity, grab it by the throat and bring it home. Having said that the following are some of things that you should take into account before quitting your job to start your online business:

- **Expenses** – It's a good idea to calculate your entire expenses for up to a year and set aside the money to cover them before quitting your job. These expenses will include the costs of basic things like: shelter, food, clothing, transportation, and health insurance. Now in regards to health insurance you may have to forego health insurance initially because of the high costs associated with independently insuring yourself. Perhaps you can get around this if you are married and your spouse is able to put you on their company's insurance plan.

  In addition, you also have to take into account the expenses that will be involved in starting and operating your online business and include them in your overall budget. This will importantly include money to build a website and marketing dollars. It will also include working capital to run your business. If you don't have enough money in your savings to put aside for your expenses as I just mentioned in the last chapter perhaps you can get your family and friends to invest in your online business to help you raise the necessary funds.

- **Your willingness to sacrifice and your risk tolerance** – Starting a business involves making an incredible amount of sacrifices and anyone who tells you anything different is lying to you. You will sacrifice your time, your money and your energy. You will probably encounter roller coaster income that goes up and down until you figure how to make your business income predictable, but hey this is part of the journey. Can you stomach this? Really, you have to truthfully answer that question before quitting your job and giving up the comforts of receiving a predictable paycheck. Some people have a big aversion to risk of any kind even if it involves a calculated risk. You must determine if you are one of those types of people before sacrificing your paycheck for the unknown.

- **Testing your business idea out first before making the leap**
  Your business idea may look good drawn up on the back of a napkin and in your analysis may be fundamentally a sound one, but until it's proven you really have nothing but your idea. You have no product; no demand, no customers and you are not making any money from it. The only way to find out if your particular business idea works is by testing it out.

You don't have to quit your job to find out if you have a workable idea that makes money so don't do it. Once you have a proven business concept and you see that it generates a sufficient enough revenue stream for you and it's scalable, it makes it easier for you to decide whether or not to quit your job.

- **Feedback from others** – It's a good idea to get feedback from others that you respect or if possible who have already been down the entrepreneurial road you are trying to travel before quitting your job. The purpose of listening to this feedback is to hear other perspectives and viewpoints beside your own. Maybe you will come across additional ideas in which you can build upon or maybe you will discover through feedback that you forgot to take in consideration something major that could possibly affect and determine whether you are heading in the right direction or whether you succeed or not.

I have a few entrepreneurs who are in my network that I like to bounce ideas off of just to see what they think. I then use this feedback if it applies to refine my ideas and strategies. Feedback is essential and it is important that you get some before deciding to quit your job.

- **Your support system** – Before deciding to quit your job to start your online business you want to make sure that the people who make up your support system and will be directly impacted by your decision have a great understanding of the challenges that lie ahead and they are on board with it, especially if they are your significant other. They have to understand that sacrifices will have to be made in all areas and they will experience a bit of discomfort that they are probably not use to.

  If you don't have their full support it will be difficult for you to devote the maximum amount of energy needed to run and operate your business while also managing the undue stress in your relationship resulting from your decision to quit your job. The distraction may even become big enough that you might have to dissolve your relationship completely.

- **Your fears–** The thought of quitting your job can evoke and bring to the surface fears that you might have in regards to taking that big step. It is best that you first deal with those fears head on before quitting your job because if you don't they will overwhelm you and sabotage your chances to be successful.

What is fear anyway? Fear is nothing more than false expectations appearing real.

One of the first steps that you can take in overcoming your fears is to first acknowledge them. Once you have acknowledged them you have to then define what they are. Once you have defined what they are the next step is to address them and work to put what you fear in the proper context so that you are able to manage that fear or totally eliminate it from your mind. For example, you may have the fear of losing a so called "secure" paycheck.

However, if you go a lot deeper you will realize this fear originates from how you view money. Your view of money is that it's scarce and hard to come by, so you fear losing it. You also believe that the only way that you can get money is by someone else's hand. You lack the belief that you can get it yourself without having to work at a job. When someone else issues you a check you feel "secure".

Now the way that you can confront this paralyzing fear of losing a so called "secure" paycheck is by challenging your scarcity beliefs and views about money. You challenge your beliefs and change them with strong evidence that supports a new line of thought. For example, your false evidence suggests that money is scarce, but the reality is that it is not. Money is abundant, just look around you it is everywhere. Go to any place of commerce and you will see money rapidly exchanging hands, from buyer to seller and from seller to buyer.

The money in the universe is not confined and limited to your paycheck, and the evidence that I've just presented proves that point. If you start seeing money as abundant you will abolish your scarcity mentality as well as your fear of losing a so called "secure" paycheck. By the way security is nothing more than an illusion.

The evidence also strongly suggests that you can in fact live and function without a job if you tap into the strength of your inner self and the laws of nature and the universe. Just look at animals in their natural state. Do they get what they need to survive like food, shelter etc.? Do they depend on receiving a paycheck from someone for their survival? Of course not! Then why should you? The reason why they don't and you do is because you've been manipulated by the powers to be to live in an unnatural state of total dependence in order to control you.

Don't you think that it's time for you to revert back to your natural state of self sufficiency and the power to control your own destiny? Well, if you do, you have to eliminate those fears that you can't do for yourself and you can't live or function without a paycheck.

Conclusion

There are many challenges that you will encounter when transforming yourself from a person who thinks and acts like an employee to a person who is a full-fledged online entrepreneur. Hopefully, the lessons and the information that I have provided throughout this book will aid you as proceed forward in your entrepreneurial journey. If you need further assistance I offer one on one coaching through my Entrepreneur Mentorship Program. For more information and a **Free Consultation** just visit http://www.makeprofitseasy.com.

Good luck and I wish you much success with your entrepreneurial endeavors.

Omar Johnson

Other Books Available By Author On Kindle, Audio and Paperback

The Killer Instinct: How To Master It and Achieve Anything That You Want

Winning Habits: Getting Rid of A Loser's Mentality

Conquering Your Fears

Passive Income: Stop Working Hard For Your Money And Let Your Money Work Hard For You

How To Create A Profitable Ezine From Scratch

The Secrets Of Making $10,000 on Ebay in 30 Days

The Complete Guide To Investing in Gold And Silver: Surviving The Great Economic Depression

How To Sell Any Product Online:"Secrets of The Killer Sales Letter"

How To Make A Fortune Using The Public Domain

Search Engine Domination: The Ultimate Secrets To Increasing Your Website's Visibility And Making A Ton Of Cash

Creative Real Estate Investing Strategies And Tips

How to Make Money Online:"The Savvy Entrepreneur's Guide To Financial Freedom"

How to Overcome Your Self-Limiting Beliefs & Achieve Anything You Want

The Secrets of Finding The Perfect Ghostwriter For Your Book

The Creative Real Estate Marketing Equation: Motivated Sellers + Motivated Buyers = $

How To Start An Online Business With Less Than $200

How To Market Your Business Online and Offline

Money Blueprint: The Secrets To Creating Instant Wealth

Affiliate Cash: How To Make Money As An Affiliate Marketer

How To Promote Market And Sell Your Kindle Book

AudioBook Profits: How To Make Money by Turning Your Kindle, Paperback and Hardcover Book into Audio.

The Fine Art of Writing The Next Best Seller on Kindle

Fast Cash: 9 Amazing Ways To Make Money Without Having To Work At A Job

Money Magnet: How to use the Laws of the Universe to Attract Money into Your Life

Hypnotic Influence: How To Create A Cult Like Following For Anything That You Do

Jobless Cash: How to Make Money if You're Unemployed or Just Plain Tired of Working for Someone Else

The Art Of Manipulation: How To Get Anybody To Do Anything That You Want